PIC DU MIDI, NAVARRE

SHAKESPEARE'S

COMEDY OF

LOVE'S LABOUR'S LOST

EDITED, WITH NOTES

BY

WILLIAM J. ROLFE, Litt.D.

FORMERLY HEAD MASTER OF THE HIGH SCHOOL,
CAMBRIDGE, MASS.

ILLUSTRATED

NEW YORK ·:· CINCINNATI ·:· CHICAGO
AMERICAN BOOK COMPANY

PREFACE

THIS play, originally edited by me in 1882, is now very carefully revised on the same general plan as the earlier volumes of the new series.

Dr. Furness's "New Variorum" edition of the play did not appear until after my revised copy had gone to the printer, but I have fortunately been able to make some use of it in reading the proofs of my Notes.

CONTENTS

DULL, COSTARD AND JAQUENETTA

COSTUMES OF THE PERIOD

INTRODUCTION TO LOVE'S LABOUR'S LOST

THE HISTORY OF THE PLAY

THE earliest edition of *Love's Labour's Lost* that has come down to us is a quarto published in 1598, the title-page of which describes it as "a pleasant conceited comedie . . . presented before her Highnes this last Christmas," and as "by W. Shakespere."

The earliest mention of the play that has been discovered is in the following lines from a poem entitled *Alba, or the Months Mind of a Melancholy Lover*, by "R. T. Gentleman" (Robert Tofte), published in 1598 : —

> " *Love's Labour Lost* I once did see, a Play
> Y-cleped so, so called to my paine.
> Which I to heare to my small Ioy did stay,
> Giving attendance on my froward Dame :
>   My misgiving minde presaging to me ill,
>   Yet was I drawne to see it 'gainst my will.
>
>   *   *   *   *   *   *
>
> Each Actor plaid in cunning wise his part,
> But chiefly Those entrapt in Cupids snare ;
> Yet All was fained, 't was not from the hart,
> They seemde to grieve, but yet they felt no care :
>   'T was I that Griefe (indeed) did beare in brest,
>   The others did but make a show in Iest."

The play is also included in Francis Meres's famous list of Shakespeare's works in his *Palladis Tamia*, printed in 1598.

It was doubtless written as early as 1591, and some critics date it two or three years earlier — Furnivall in 1588-89, and Grant White as " probably not later than 1588."

Among the marks of early style may be mentioned : the introduction of well-known old characters (besides " the Nine Worthies," we have what Biron calls " the pedant, the braggart, the hedge priest, the fool, and the boy ") ; the observance of the " unities " ; the abundance of rhyme ; the doggerel ; the sonnets (occasionally as speeches) ; the alliteration, or " affecting the letter," as Holofernes calls it ; the quibbles, antitheses, repartees, " the sparkles of wit, like a blaze of fireworks " (Schlegel) ; the proverbial expressions ; the peculiar and pedantic **grammatical** constructions ; the words used in their native forms; the display of learning; the pairs of characters; the disguising and changing of persons; the chorus-like, alternate answers; the strained dialogue, etc. It is "a play of conversation and situation" (Furnivall), in which "depth of characterization is subordinate to elegance and sprightliness of dialogue" (Staunton).

The play is poorly printed in both the quarto and the folio, and the repetition of sundry typographical errors proves that the latter was set up from a copy of the former. There are, however, variations in the two texts which indicate that the editors of the folio were occasionally indebted to some other authority than the quarto.

The edition of 1598 is evidently, as the title-page informs us, "newly corrected and augmented." In two instances a lucky blunder of the printer has preserved the original form of a passage together with the revised version — the only such illustrations of the dramatist "in the workshop" that are to be found in all his works. Elsewhere we have examples of early and later composition in different passages of a play, but never in the same passage.

In Biron's long speech (iv. 3. 287 fol.) we have these lines : [1]—

> "For when would you, my lord, — or you, — or you, —
> Have found the ground of study's excellence

[1] I print the passages here for the convenience of the reader in comparing them instead of referring him to the text of the play.

Without the beauty of a woman's face?
From women's eyes this doctrine I derive :
They are the ground, the books, the academes,
From whence doth spring the true Promethean fire.

* * * * * *

For where is any author in the world
Teaches such beauty as a woman's eye ?
Learning is but an adjunct to ourself,
And where we are our learning likewise is ;
Then when ourselves we see in ladies' eyes,
Do we not likewise see our learning there ?
O, we have made a vow to study, lords,
And in that vow we have forsworn our books."

This belongs to the play as first written. Some editors
strike it out ; but it seems better (as I have done in this
edition) to retain it enclosed in brackets. It re-appears
in the revision of the speech thus : —

"For when would you, my liege, — or you, — or you, —
In leaden contemplation have found out
Such fiery numbers as the prompting eyes
Of beauty's tutors have enrich'd you with ?

* * * * * *

Never durst poet touch a pen to write
Until his ink were temper'd with Love's sighs;
O, then his lines would ravish savage ears
And plant in tyrants mild humility !
From women's eyes this doctrine I derive :
They sparkle still the right Promethean fire;
They are the books, the arts, the academes,
That show, contain, and nourish all the world,
Else none at all in aught proves excellent.
Then fools you were these women to **forswear,**

> Or, keeping what is sworn, you will prove fools.
> For wisdom's sake, a word that all men love,
> Or for love's sake, a word that loves all men,
> Or for men's sake, the authors of these women,
> Or women's sake, by whom we men are men,
> Let us once lose our oaths to find ourselves,
> Or else we lose ourselves to keep our oaths."

Again, in v. 2. 821 fol., we find this bit of the original play: —

> " *Biron.*   And what to me, my love? and what to me?
>   *Rosaline.*   You must be purged too, your sins are rank,
> You are attaint with faults and perjury;
> Therefore if you my favour mean to get,
> A twelvemonth shall you spend, and never rest,
> But seek the weary beds of people sick."

In the revision Biron's question is transferred to Dumain: " But what to me, my love? but what to me? " and the passage is altered and expanded thus: —

> " *Biron.*   Studies my lady? mistress, look on me;
> Behold the window of my heart, mine eye,
> What humble suit attends thy answer there;
> Impose some service on me for thy love.
>   *Rosaline.*   Oft have I heard of you, my Lord Biron,
> Before I saw you; and the world's large tongue
> Proclaims you for a man replete with mocks,
> Full of comparisons and wounding flouts,
> Which you on all estates will execute
> That lie within the mercy of your wit.
> To weed this wormwood from your fruitful brain,
> And therewithal to win me, if you please, —
> Without the which I am not to be won, —

> You shall this twelvemonth term from day to day
> Visit the speechless sick, and still converse
> With groaning wretches; and your task shall be,
> With all the fierce endeavour of your wit
> To enforce the pained impotent to smile."

One or two critics — apparently from a desire to save the credit of the player editors of the folio, whatever be the damage to that of the author — seriously tell us that there is no mixing up of early and later work in these passages, but that the folio gives us the text as Shakespeare wrote or revised it. It is generally agreed, however, that fragments of the original text are unquestionably retained in the revised version. In the first two passages quoted the correction, as Herford says, "has merely served to heighten the vigour of the phrasing;" but the third "throws the divergences of the Shakespeare of 1597 from the Shakespeare of eight years earlier into glaring relief. The earlier version of Rosaline's compact with Biron is singularly jejune. The past mistress of quips and cranks seems to take up the rôle of moral censor as a new phase in the game of outwitting the lords, and to impose her penalty by way of flinging a last decisive shot at her adversary. In the latter version she has passed, like the princess, into a serious and feeling mood (announced to the reader by Biron's question, 'Studies my lady?'), and the demand, before petulantly tossed at him in somewhat jerky iambics, is now gravely formulated in lines of subtly varied movement and eloquently rounded phrase, and with a moral dignity for which certainly nothing in her previous bearing prepares us. But then Shakespeare, when he thus 'corrected,' was already the creator of Portia."

THE SOURCES OF THE PLOT

The plot of the play, so far as we know, was original with Shakespeare. Dowden remarks: "The play is precisely such a one as a clever young man might imagine, who had come lately from the country — with its 'daisies pied and violets blue,' its 'merry larks,' its maidens who 'bleach their summer smocks,' its pompous parish schoolmaster and its dull constable (a great public official in his own eyes) — to the town, where he was surrounded by more brilliant unrealities, and affectations of dress, of manner, of language, and of ideas. *Love's Labour's Lost* is a dramatic plea on behalf of nature and of common-sense, against all that is unreal and affected."

Grant White, however, believes that the dramatist was indebted to some lost original. He says: "That the play is founded upon some older work, its undramatic character, its needless fulness of detail, its air of artificial romance, and the attribution of particular personal traits — such as black eyes and a dark complexion to one, great size to another, and a face pitted with the small-pox to another of the ladies, and the merely incidental hints that one of the king's friends is an officer in the army and extremely youthful — seem unmistakable evidence; and that the story is of French origin is as clearly shown by the nationality of the titles, the Gallicism of calling a love-letter a *capon*, the appearance of the strong French negative *point* twice, and the use of *seigneur* instead of *signior*."[1]

Rev. Joseph Hunter, in his *New Illustrations* (vol. i. p. 256), suggests that the poet may have got a hint from Monstrelet's *Chronicles*, according to which Charles, King of Navarre, surrendered to the King of France the castle of Cherbourg, the county of Evreux, and other lordships for the Duchy of Nemours and a promise of 200,000 gold crowns. The hero of the play is the King of Navarre, and Sidney Lee has shown (*Gentleman's Magazine*, October, 1880) that Biron and Longaville bear the names of the two most strenuous supporters of the real king, and that the name Dumain is an Anglicized form of that of the Duc de Maine or Mayenne, who was so often mentioned in popular accounts of French affairs in connection with Navarre that Shakespeare was led to number him also among the king's supporters. Mothe or La Mothe, from whom the page perhaps gets his name, was a French ambassador long popular in London. M. Le Mot is a courtier

---

[1] This spelling occurs only in i. 2. 10 ("Why tough senior?"), where the word is not a title. In iii. 1. 177 ("senior-junior") it is "signior" in the early eds. It occurs as a title only in i. 1. 185 and iii. 1. 127, where it is "signior" in all the early eds. In the *C. of E.*, where no French influence can be suspected, we find in v. 1. 422 ("We 'll draw cuts for the senior") "signior," "signeor," and "signeur." In *Rich. III.*, iv. 4. 36, "seniory" (of age) is "signeurie" and "signorie."

n Chapman's *Humorous Day's Mirth,* 1599, and is lluded to in Middleton's *Blurt, Master Constable,* 1602. Armado is a caricature of a half-crazed Spaniard known as "fantastical Monarcho," who for many years hung about the Court of Elizabeth. Sundry other persons and topics of the time are alluded to in the play.

Monarcho's "Epitaph," written by Churchyard (1580), refers to him as a compound of folly and wit, " grave of looks and father-like of face," who uttered "strange talk" before strangers, not inclined to mirth, but " well disposed if any prince took pleasure in the mirth he made " — or " loved to hear him lie," as the King says of Armado. Churchyard (quoted by Herford) apostrophizes him thus : —

> " Thy climbing mind aspir'd beyond the stars ;
> Thy lofty style no earthly title bore ;
> Thy wits would seem to see through peace and wars,
> Thy taunting tongue was pleasant, sharp, and sore,
> And tho' thy pride and pomp was somewhat vain
> The Monarch had a deep-discoursing brain."

" But," as Herford adds, " Armado need not be in any sense a *portrait* of Monarcho, any more than of John Lyly, Antonio Perez, or Philip II., with whom different critics have confidently identified him." Neither is there any ground for supposing that in Holofernes the dramatist caricatured John Florio, the eminent Italian scholar and translator of Montaigne ; nor has Rosaline though a brunette any relationship to the " dark lady " of the *Sonnets,* as certain critics have assumed. The

satire in the play is nowise personal, but is evidently
directed against the general pedantry and literary
affectations of the times.

GENERAL COMMENTS ON THE PLAY

The best critics take the view of the play which has just
been expressed.   Coleridge remarks : " The characters
are either impersonated out of Shakspeare's own multi-
formity by imaginative self-position, or out of such as a
country town and schoolboy's observation might supply
— the curate, the schoolmaster, the Armado (who even
in my time was not extinct in the cheaper inns of North
Wales), and so on.   The satire is chiefly on follies of
words.   Biron and Rosaline are evidently the pre-
existent state of Benedick and Beatrice, and so, perhaps,
is Boyet of Lafeu, and Costard of the Tapster in *Measure for Measure ;* and the frequency of the rhymes, the
sweetness as well as the smoothness of the metre, and
the number of acute and fancifully illustrated aphorisms,
are all as they ought to be in a poet's youth.   True
genius begins by generalizing and condensing ; it ends
in realizing and expanding.   It first collects the seeds.

" Yet if this juvenile drama had been the only one
extant of our Shakspeare, and we possessed the tradition
only of his riper works, or accounts of them in writers
who had not even mentioned this play, how many of
Shakspeare's characteristic features might we not still
have discovered in *Love's Labour's Lost,* though as in a
portrait taken of him in his boyhood !

"I can never sufficiently admire the wonderful activity of thought throughout the whole of the first scene of the play, rendered natural, as it is, by the choice of the characters, and the whimsical determination on which the drama is founded. A whimsical determination certainly; yet not altogether so very improbable to those who are conversant in the history of the Middle Ages, with their Courts of Love, and all that lighter drapery of chivalry, which engaged even mighty kings with a sort of serio-comic interest, and may well be supposed to have occupied more completely the smaller princes, at a time when the noble's or prince's court contained the only theatre of the domain or principality. This sort of story, too, was admirably suited to Shakspeare's times, when the English court was still the foster-mother of the state and the muses; and when, in consequence, the courtiers, and men of rank and fashion, affected a display of wit, point, and sententious observation that would be deemed intolerable at present, but in which a hundred years of controversy, involving every great political, and every dear domestic, interest, had trained all but the lowest classes to participate. . . .

"Hence the comic matter chosen in the first instance is a ridiculous imitation or apery of this constant striving after logical precision, and subtle opposition of thoughts, together with a making the most of every conception or image, by expressing it under the least expected property belonging to it, and this, again, rendered specially absurd by being applied to the most current subjects and occurrences.   The phrases and modes of combination in argument were caught by the most ignorant from the custom of the age, and their ridiculous misapplication of them is most amusingly exhibited in Costard; whilst examples suited only to the gravest propositions and impersonations, or apostrophes to abstract thoughts impersonated, which are in fact the natural language only of the most vehement agitations of the mind, are adopted by the coxcombry of Armado as mere artifices of ornament.

" The same kind of intellectual action is exhibited in a more serious and elevated strain in many other parts of this play.   Biron's speech at the end of the fourth act is an excellent specimen of it.   It is logic clothed in rhetoric; but observe how Shakspeare, in his twofold being of poet and philosopher, avails himself of it to convey profound truths in the most lively images — the whole remaining faithful to the character supposed to utter the lines, and the expressions themselves constituting a further development of that character."

I will add portions of Verplanck's comments on the play (in his edition of Shakespeare, 1847), which unfortunately are out of print and not accessible in many of the libraries : —

" There is a general concurrence of opinion, both traditional and critical, that this play was among Shakespeare's earliest dramatic works. . . .   Its general resemblance of style and thought to his other early works, and especially the ' frequency of the rhymes, the sweetness as well as the smoothness of the metre, and the number of acute and fancifully illustrated aphorisms,' all correspond with the idea of a youthful work; while, as in others of his early works, we also find in the personages the rudiments of characters, slightly sketched, to which he afterwards returned, and, without repeating himself, presented them again, in a varied and more individualized and living form. Thus, Biron contains within him the germs both of Benedick and of Jaques; of the one in his colloquial and mocking mood, and of the other in his graver moralities. Rosaline is (in Coleridge's phrase) 'the pre-existent state of Beatrice;' though she is as yet a Beatrice of the imagination, drawn from books or report, rather than one painted from familiar acquaintance.

"Both the characters and the dialogue are such as youthful talent might well invent, without much knowledge of real life, and would indeed be likely to invent, before the experience and observation of varied society. The comedy presents a picture, not of the true everyday life of the great or the beautiful, but exhibits groups of such brilliant personages as they might be supposed to appear in the artificial conversation, the elaborate and continual effort to surprise or dazzle by wit or elegance, which was the prevailing taste of the age, in its literature, its poetry, and even its pulpit; and in which the nobles and beauties of the day were accustomed to array themselves for exhibition, as in their state attire, for occasions of display. All this, when the leading idea was once caught, was quite within the reach of the young poet to imitate or surpass, with little or no personal knowledge of aristocratic — or what would now be termed fashionable — society. English literature, a century later, afforded a striking example of the success of a very young author in carrying to its perfection a similar affectation of artificial wit, and studied conversational brilliancy — I mean Congreve, whose comedies, the admiration of their own age, for their fertility of fantastically gay dialogue, bright conceits, and witty repartees, are still read for their abundance of lively imagery and play of language, the 'reciprocation of conceits and the clash of wit,'— although the personages of his scene, and all that they do and think, are wholly remote from the truth, the feeling, and the manners of real life. These productions, so remarkable in their way, were written before Congreve's twenty-fifth year ; and his first and most brilliant comedy (*The Old Bachelor*) was acted when he was yet a minor. His talent, thus early ripe, did not afterwards expand or refine itself into the nobler power of teaching 'the morals of the heart,' nor even into the delightful gift of embodying the passing scenes of real life in graphic and durable pictures. But his writings afford a memorable proof how soon the graces and brilliant effects of mere intellect can be acquired, while those works of genius which require the co-operation and the knowledge of man's moral nature are of slower and later growth.

"This comedy, then, marks the transition of Shakespeare's mind through the Congreve character of invention and dialogue; that of lively and artificial brilliancy — a region in which he did not long loiter —

> "'But stoop'd to truth, and moraliz'd his song.'

"These remarks apply to the general contexture of the comedy, and the greater part of the dialogue. But it must not be overlooked that the whole is not the work of a mere boy. It had been played before Queen Elizabeth, according to the title-page of the edition of 1598, 'this last Christmas,' and had been 'newly corrected and augmented.' . . . It does not imply any great presumption of criticism, or demand peculiar delicacy of discrimination, to separate many of the acknowledged additions from the lighter and less valuable materials in which they are inserted. Rosaline's character of Biron in the second act, and her dialogue with him at the winding up of the drama, and Biron's speeches in the first and at the end of the fourth act, are among the passages which appropriate themselves at once to the period of the composition of the *Merchant of Venice*, not less in the mood of thought than in the peculiar poetic style and melody.

"The story itself is but slight, the incidents few, and the higher characters, though varied, are but sketchily drawn — at least, taking the author's own maturer style of execution in that way as the standard. There was, therefore, no very great effort of original invention in

either respect; but whatever there is, either of plot or
character, belongs to the author alone : for the diligence
of the critics and antiquarians who have been most successful in tracing out the rough materials of romance,
tradition, or history used by Shakespeare for the construction of his dramas, has entirely failed in discover-
ing any thing of the kind in any older author, native or
foreign, to which he could have been indebted on this
occasion.   It is well worthy of remark that Shakespeare,
in his earlier works, bestowed more of the labour of invention upon his plot and incidents than he generally
did afterwards, when he usually selected known personages, to whom and to the outline of whose story the
popular mind was already somewhat familiar — thus,
probably quite unconsciously, adopting from his own
experience the usage of the great Greek dramatists.   It
may be that the impress of reality, which the circum-
stance of familiar names and events lends to the drama,
more than compensated for any pleasure that mere
novelty of incident could give either to the author or
his audience.   But, in his characters of broad humour,
Shakespeare is here, as he always is, original and in-
ventive.   Although the Pedant and the Braggart are
characters familiar to the old Italian stage, yet if the
dramatist derived the general notion of such personages, as fitted for stage effect, from any Italian source
(for the presumption is but remote), still he assuredly
painted them and their affectations from the life ; these
being characters, as Coleridge justly observes, which

'a country town and a schoolboy's observation might supply.'

"All the personages of broader humour, in spite of their extravagances and droll absurdities, have still an air of truth, a solidity of effect, which at once indicates that, however heightened and exaggerated, still they came upon the stage from the real world, and not from the author's fancy; and this solidity and reality tend to give a more unreal and shadowy tone to the other and more courtly and poetic personages of the comedy. Such a remark can apply only to Shakespeare's very early dramatic works. The other comic creations of the second stage of the poet's career — Launcelot Gobbo, or Falstaff — do not command the temporary illusion of the stage more than the nobler personages with whom they are contrasted. Juliet is as true and real as her Nurse."

LOVE'S LABOUR 'S LOST

DRAMATIS PERSONÆ

FERDINAND, King of Navarre.
BIRON,
LONGAVILLE, } lords attending on the King.
DUMAIN,
BOYET, } lords attending on the Princess of France.
MERCADE,
DON ADRIANO DE ARMADO, a fantastical Spaniard.
SIR NATHANIEL, a curate.
HOLOFERNES, a schoolmaster.
DULL, a constable.
COSTARD, a clown.
MOTH, page to Armado.
A Forester.

THE PRINCESS OF FRANCE.
ROSALINE,
MARIA, } ladies attending on the Princess.
KATHERINE,
JAQUENETTA, a country wench.

Lords, Attendants, etc.

SCENE: *Navarre.*

"THY CURIOUS-KNOTTED GARDEN"

ACT I

SCENE I. *The King of Navarre's Park*

Enter FERDINAND, *King of Navarre*, BIRON, LONGA-
VILLE, *and* DUMAIN

King. Let fame, that all hunt after in their lives,
Live register'd upon our brazen tombs,
And then grace us in the disgrace of death;
When, spite of cormorant devouring Time,
The endeavour of this present breath may buy
That honour which shall bate his scythe's keen edge
And make us heirs of all eternity.

Therefore, brave conquerors, — for so you are
That war against your own affections
And the huge army of the world's desires,—   10
Our late edict shall strongly stand in force.
Navarre shall be the wonder of the world;
Our court shall be a little Academe,
Still and contemplative in living art.
You three, Biron, Dumain, and Longaville,
Have sworn for three years' term to live with me
My fellow-scholars, and to keep those statutes
That are recorded in this schedule here.
Your oaths are pass'd; and now subscribe your
          names,
That his own hand may strike his honour down   20
That violates the smallest branch herein.
If you are arm'd to do as sworn to do,
Subscribe to your deep oaths, and keep it too.
     Longaville. I am resolv'd; 't is but a three years'
          fast.
The mind shall banquet, though the body pine.
Fat paunches have lean pates, and dainty bits
Make rich the ribs but bankrupt quite the wits.
     Dumain. My loving lord, Dumain is mortified;
The grosser manner of these world's delights
He throws upon the gross world's baser slaves.   30
To love, to wealth, to pomp, I pine and die,
With all these living in philosophy.
     Biron. I can but say their protestation over;
So much, dear liege, I have already sworn,

That is, to live and study here three years.
But there are other strict observances ;
As, not to see a woman in that term,
Which I hope well is not enrolled there ;
And one day in a week to touch no food,
And but one meal on every day beside,   40
The which I hope is not enrolled there ;
And then, to sleep but three hours in the night,
And not be seen to wink of all the day —
When I was wont to think no harm all night,
And make a dark night too of half the day, —
Which I hope well is not enrolled there.
O, these are barren tasks, too hard to keep,
Not to see ladies, study, fast, not sleep !
   King. Your oath is pass'd to pass away from
     these.
   Biron. Let me say no, my liege, an if you please ; 50
I only swore to study with your grace,
And stay here in your court for three years' space.
   Longaville. You swore to that, Biron, and to the
     rest.
   Biron. By yea and nay, sir, then I swore in jest.
What is the end of study? let me know.
   King. Why, that to know which else we should not
     know.
   Biron. Things hid and barr'd, you mean, from com-
     mon sense ?
   King. Ay, that is study's godlike recompense.
   Biron. Come on, then ; I will swear to study so

To know the thing I am forbid to know: 60
As thus, — to study where I well may dine,
  When I to feast expressly am forbid;
Or study where to meet some mistress fine,
  When mistresses from common sense are hid;
Or, having sworn too hard a keeping oath,
Study to break it and not break my troth.
If study's gain be thus, and this be so,
Study knows that which yet it doth not know.
Swear me to this, and I will ne'er say no.

  King. These be the stops that hinder study quite, 70
And train our intellects to vain delight.

  Biron. Why, all delights are vain, and that most vain
Which with pain purchas'd doth inherit pain;
As, painfully to pore upon a book
  To seek the light of truth, while truth the while
Doth falsely blind the eyesight of his look.

  Light seeking light doth light of light beguile;
So, ere you find where light in darkness lies,
Your light grows dark by losing of your eyes.
Study me how to please the eye indeed 80
  By fixing it upon a fairer eye,
Who dazzling so, that eye shall be his heed
  And give him light that it was blinded by.
Study is like the heaven's glorious sun,
  That will not be deep-search'd with saucy looks;
Small have continual plodders ever won
  Save base authority from others' books.
These earthly godfathers of heaven's lights,

That give a name to every fixed star,
Have no more profit of their shining nights   90
    Than those that walk and wot not what they are.
Too much to know is to know nought but fame;
And every godfather can give a name.

    King. How well he's read, to reason against reading!

    Dumain. Proceeded well, to stop all good proceeding!

    Longaville. He weeds the corn and still lets grow the weeding.

    Biron. The spring is near when green geese are a-breeding.

    Dumain. How follows that?

    Biron.   Fit in his place and time.

    Dumain. In reason nothing.

    Biron.   Something then in rhyme.

    King. Biron is like an envious sneaping frost   100
That bites the first-born infants of the spring.

    Biron. Well, say I am; why should proud summer boast
Before the birds have any cause to sing?
Why should I joy in an abortive birth?
    At Christmas I no more desire a rose
Than wish a snow in May's new-fangled shows,
    But like of each thing that in season grows.
So you, to study now it is too late,
Climb o'er the house to unlock the little gate.

    King. Well, sit you out. Go home, Biron; adieu!

    Biron. No, my good lord, I have sworn to stay with you;   111

And though I have for barbarism spoke more
   Than for that angel knowledge you can say,
Yet confident I 'll keep what I have swore,
   And bide the penance of each three years' day.
Give me the paper; let me read the same,
And to the strict'st decrees I 'll write my name.

   King. How well this yielding rescues thee from
       shame!

   Biron. [Reads] '*Item, That no woman shall come
within a mile of my court*—' Hath this been proclaimed?   121

   Longaville. Four days ago.

   Biron. Let 's see the penalty.   [Reads] '*On pain
of losing her tongue.*' — Who devised this penalty?

   Longaville. Marry, that did I.

   Biron. Sweet lord, and why?

   Longaville. To fright them hence with that dread
       penalty.

   Biron. A dangerous law against gentility!

   [Reads] '*Item, If any man be seen to talk with a
woman within the term of three years, he shall endure
such public shame as the rest of the court can possibly
devise.*'   132

This article, my liege, yourself must break;
   For well you know here comes in embassy
The French king's daughter with yourself to speak—
   A maid of grace and complete majesty—
About surrender up of Aquitaine
   To her decrepit, sick, and bedrid father.

Therefore this article is made in vain,
  Or vainly comes the admired princess hither.   140
  King. What say you, lords? why, this was quite
    forgot.
  Biron. So study evermore is overshot.
While it doth study to have what it would,
It doth forget to do the thing it should;
And when it hath the thing it hunteth most,
'T is won as towns with fire, so won, so lost.
  King. We must of force dispense with this decree;
She must lie here on mere necessity.
  Biron. Necessity will make us all forsworn
  Three thousand times within this three years' space;
For every man with his affects is born,   151
  Not by might master'd, but by special grace.
If I break faith, this word shall speak for me:
I am forsworn on mere necessity. —
So to the laws at large I write my name;   [*Subscribes.*
  And he that breaks them in the least degree
Stands in attainder of eternal shame.
  Suggestions are to others as to me;
But I believe, although I seem so loath,
I am the last that will last keep his oath.   160
But is there no quick recreation granted?
  King. Ay, that there is. Our court, you know, is
    haunted
  With a refined traveller of Spain;
A man in all the world's new fashion planted,
  That hath a mint of phrases in his brain;

One whom the music of his own vain tongue
    Doth ravish like enchanting harmony;
A man of complements, whom right and wrong
    Have chose as umpire of their mutiny.
This child of fancy, that Armado hight,   170
    For interim to our studies shall relate
In high-born words the worth of many a knight
    From tawny Spain lost in the world's debate.
How you delight, my lords, I know not, I,
But, I protest, I love to hear him lie,
And I will use him for my minstrelsy.
    Biron. Armado is a most illustrious wight,
A man of fire-new words, fashion's own knight.
    Longaville. Costard the swain and he shall be our
        sport;
And so to study, three years is but short.   180

Enter DULL *with a letter, and* COSTARD

    Dull. Which is the duke's own person?
    Biron. This, fellow; what wouldst?
    Dull. I myself reprehend his own person, for I
am his grace's tharborough; but I would see his own
person in flesh and blood.
    Biron. This is he.
    Dull. Signior Arme — Arme — commends you.
There's villany abroad; this letter will tell you
more.
    Costard. Sir, the contempts thereof are as touch-
ing me.   191

King. A letter from the magnificent Armado.

Biron. How low soever the matter, I hope in God for high words.

Longaville. A high hope for a low having; God grant us patience!

Biron. To hear? or forbear laughing?

Longaville. To hear meekly, sir, and to laugh moderately; or to forbear both.

Biron. Well, sir, be it as the style shall give us cause to climb in the merriness.   201

Costard. The matter is to me, sir, as concerning Jaquenetta. The manner of it is, I was taken with the manner.

Biron. In what manner?

Costard. In manner and form following, sir; all those three: I was seen with her in the manor-house, sitting with her upon the form, and taken following her into the park, which, put together, is in manner and form following. Now, sir, for the manner, — it is the manner of a man to speak to a woman; for the form, — in some form.   212

Biron. For the following, sir?

Costard. As it shall follow in my correction; and God defend the right!

King. Will you hear this letter with attention?

Biron. As we would hear an oracle.

Costard. Such is the simplicity of man to hearken after the flesh.

King. [Reads] ' *Great deputy, the welkin's vicege-*

*rent and sole dominator of Navarre, my soul's earth's
god, and body's fostering patron.'*   222

   Costard. Not a word of Costard yet.

   King. [Reads] ' *So it is,*' —

   Costard. It may be so; but if he say it is so, he
is, in telling true, but so.

   King. Peace!

   Costard. Be to me, and every man that dares not
fight!

   King. No words!   230

   Costard. Of other men's secrets, I beseech you.

   King. [Reads] ' *So it is, besieged with sable-coloured
melancholy, I did commend the black-oppressing humour
to the most wholesome physic of thy health-giving air,
and, as I am a gentleman, betook myself to walk.   The
time when?   About the sixth hour, when beasts most
graze, birds best peck, and men sit down to that nour-
ishment which is called supper; so much for the time
when.   Now for the ground which, — which, I mean,
I walked upon; it is ycleped thy park.   Then for the* 240
*place where, — where, I mean, I did encounter that
obscene and most preposterous event that draweth from
my snow-white pen the ebon-coloured ink, which here
thou viewest, beholdest, surveyest, or seest; — but to the
place where; it standeth north-north-east and by east
from the west corner of thy curious-knotted garden.
There did I see that low-spirited swain, that base min-
now of thy mirth,*' —

   Costard. Me.

King. [Reads] '*that unlettered small-knowing soul,*'—   251

Costard. Me.

King. [Reads] '*that shallow vassal,*' —

Costard. Still me.

King. [Reads] '*which, as I remember, hight Costard,*' —

Costard. O, me!

King. [Reads] '*sorted and consorted, contrary to thy established proclaimed edict and continent canon, with* — *with* — *O, with* — *but with this I passion to say wherewith,*' —

Costard. With a wench.   262

King. [Reads] '*with a child of our grandmother Eve, a female; or, for thy more sweet understanding, a woman. Him I, as my ever-esteemed duty pricks me on, have sent to thee, to receive the meed of punishment, by thy sweet grace's officer, Anthony Dull, a man of good repute, carriage, bearing, and estimation.*'

Dull. Me, an 't shall please you; I am Anthony Dull.   270

King. [Reads] '*For Jaquenetta,* — *so is the weaker vessel called which I apprehended with the aforesaid swain,* — *I keep her as a vessel of thy law's fury, and shall, at the least of thy sweet notice, bring her to trial. Thine, in all compliments of devoted and heart-burning heat of duty,*   DON ADRIANO DE ARMADO.*'

Biron. This is not so well as I looked for, but the best that ever I heard.

King. Ay, the best for the worst. — But, sirrah, what say you to this?   280

Costard. Sir, I confess the wench.

King. Did you hear the proclamation?

Costard. I do confess much of the hearing it, but little of the marking of it.

King. It was proclaimed a year's imprisonment, to be taken with a wench.

Costard. I was taken with none, sir; I was taken with a damosel.

King. Well, it was proclaimed damosel.

Costard. This was no damosel neither, sir; she was a virgin.   291

King. It is so varied too; for it was proclaimed virgin.

Costard. If it were, I deny her virginity; I was taken with a maid.

King. This maid will not serve your turn, sir.

Costard. This maid will serve my turn, sir.

King. Sir, I will pronounce your sentence: you shall fast a week with bran and water.

Costard. I had rather pray a month with mutton and porridge.   301

King. And Don Armado shall be your keeper. — My Lord Biron, see him deliver'd o'er; — And go we, lords, to put in practice that

Which each to other hath so strongly sworn.

                [*Exeunt King, Longaville, and Dumain.*

Biron. I 'll lay my head to any good man's hat,

These oaths and laws will prove an idle scorn. —
Sirrah, come on.

Costard. I suffer for the truth, sir, for true it is,
I was taken with Jaquenetta, and Jaquenetta is a
true girl; and therefore welcome the sour cup of
prosperity! Affliction may one day smile again;
and till then, sit thee down, Sorrow!   [*Exeunt.*

SCENE II. *Another Part of the Park*

Enter ARMADO *and* MOTH

Armado. Boy, what sign is it when a man of great
spirit grows melancholy?

Moth. A great sign, sir, that he will look sad.

Armado. Why, sadness is one and the selfsame
thing, dear imp.

Moth. No, no; O Lord, sir, no!

Armado. How canst thou part sadness and melancholy, my tender juvenal?

Moth. By a familiar demonstration of the working, my tough senior.   10

Armado. Why tough senior? why tough senior?

Moth. Why tender juvenal? why tender juvenal?

Armado. I spoke it, tender juvenal, as a congruent epitheton appertaining to thy young days, which
we may nominate tender.

Moth. And I, tough senior, as an appertinent
title to your old time, which we may name tough.

Armado. Pretty and apt.

Moth. How mean you, sir? I pretty, and my saying apt? or I apt, and my saying pretty?   20

Armado. Thou pretty, because little.

Moth. Little pretty, because little. Wherefore apt?

Armado. And therefore apt, because quick.

Moth. Speak you this in my praise, master?

Armado. In thy condign praise.

Moth. I will praise an eel with the same praise.

Armado. What, that an eel is ingenious?

Moth. That an eel is quick.

Armado. I do say thou art quick in answers; thou heatest my blood.   30

Moth. I am answered, sir.

Armado. I love not to be crossed.

Moth. [*Aside*] He speaks the mere contrary; crosses love not him.

Armado. I have promised to study three years with the duke.

Moth. You may do it in an hour, sir.

Armado. Impossible.

Moth. How many is one thrice told?

Armado. I am ill at reckoning; it fitteth the spirit of a tapster.   41

Moth. You are a gentleman and a gamester, sir.

Armado. I confess both; they are both the varnish of a complete man.

Moth. Then, I am sure, you know how much the gross sum of deuce-ace amounts to.

Armado. It doth amount to one more than two.

Moth. Which the base vulgar do call three.

Armado. True. 49

Moth. Why, sir, is this such a piece of study? Now here is three studied, ere you 'll thrice wink; and how easy it is to put years to the word three, and study three years in two words, the dancing horse will tell you.

Armado. A most fine figure!

Moth. [*Aside*] To prove you a cipher.

Armado. I will hereupon confess I am in love; and as it is base for a soldier to love, so am I in love with a base wench. If drawing my sword against the humour of affection would deliver me from the reprobate thought of it, I would take desire prisoner, and ransom him to any French courtier for a new-devised courtesy. I think scorn to sigh; methinks I should outswear Cupid. Comfort me, boy. What great men have been in love? 65

Moth. Hercules, master.

Armado. Most sweet Hercules!— More authority, dear boy, name more; and, sweet my child, let them be men of good repute and carriage.

Moth. Samson, master; he was a man of good carriage, great carriage, for he carried the town-gates on his back like a porter, and he was in love. 72

Armado. O well-knit Samson! strong-jointed Samson! I do excel thee in my rapier as much as thou didst me in carrying gates. I am in love too. — Who was Samson's love, my dear Moth?

Moth. A woman, master.

Armado. Of what complexion?

Moth. Of all the four, or the three, or the two, or one of the four.   80

Armado. Tell me precisely of what complexion.

Moth. Of the sea-water green, sir.

Armado. Is that one of the four complexions?

Moth. As I have read, sir; and the best of them too.

Armado. Green indeed is the colour of lovers; but to have a love of that colour, methinks Samson had small reason for it. He surely affected her for her wit.

Moth. It was so, sir; for she had a green wit.   90

Armado. My love is most immaculate white and red.

Moth. Most maculate thoughts, master, are masked under such colours.

Armado. Define, define, well-educated infant.

Moth. My father's wit and my mother's tongue, assist me!

Armado. Sweet invocation of a child; most pretty and pathetical!

Moth. If she be made of white and red,   100
      Her faults will ne'er be known,
   For blushing cheeks by faults are bred
     And fears by pale white shown;
   Then if she fear, or be to blame,
     By this you shall not know,

> For still her cheeks possess the same
>   Which native she doth owe.

A dangerous rhyme, master, against the reason of white and red.

Armado. Is there not a ballad, boy, of the King and the Beggar? 111

Moth. The world was very guilty of such a ballad some three ages since, but I think now 't is not to be found; or, if it were, it would neither serve for the writing nor the tune.

Armado. I will have that subject newly writ o'er, that I may example my digression by some mighty precedent. Boy, I do love that country girl that I took in the park with the rational hind Costard; she deserves well. 120

Moth. [*Aside*] To be whipped, — and yet a better love than my master.

Armado. Sing, boy; my spirit grows heavy in love.

Moth. And that 's great marvel, loving a light wench.

Armado. I say, sing.

Moth. Forbear till this company be past.

Enter DULL, COSTARD, *and* JAQUENETTA

Dull. Sir, the duke's pleasure is, that you keep Costard safe; and you must let him take no delight nor no penance, but he must fast three days a week. For this damsel, I must keep her at the park; she is allowed for the day-woman. Fare you well. 132

Armado. I do betray myself with blushing. — Maid!

Jaquenetta. Man!

Armado. I will visit thee at the lodge.

Jaquenetta. That 's hereby.

Armado. I know where it is situate.

Jaquenetta. Lord, how wise you are!

Armado. I will tell thee wonders.

Jaquenetta. With that face?   140

Armado. I love thee.

Jaquenetta. So I heard you say.

Armado. And so, farewell.

Jaquenetta. Fair weather after you!

Dull. Come, Jaquenetta, away!

> [*Exeunt Dull and Jaquenetta.*

Armado. Villain, thou shalt fast for thy offences
ere thou be pardoned.

Costard. Well, sir, I hope, when I do it, I shall do
it on a full stomach.

Armado. Thou shalt be heavily punished.   150

Costard. I am more bound to you than your fellows, for they are but lightly rewarded.

Armado. Take away this villain; shut him up.

Moth. Come, you transgressing slave; away!

Costard. Let me not be pent up, sir; I will fast,
being loose.

Moth. No, sir; that were fast and loose: thou
shalt to prison.

Costard. Well, if ever I do see the merry days of
desolation that I have seen, some shall see —   160

Moth. What shall some see?

Costard. Nay, nothing, Master Moth, but what they look upon. It is not for prisoners to be too silent in their words, and therefore I will say nothing. I thank God I have as little patience as another man, and therefore I can be quiet.

[*Exeunt Moth and Costard.*

Armado. I do affect the very ground, which is base, where her shoe, which is baser, guided by her foot, which is basest, doth tread. I shall be forsworn, which is a great argument of falsehood, if I 170 love. And how can that be true love which is falsely attempted? Love is a familiar; Love is a devil; there is no evil angel but Love. Yet was Samson so tempted, and he had an excellent strength; yet was Solomon so seduced, and he had a very good wit. Cupid's butt-shaft is too hard for Hercules' club, and therefore too much odds for a Spaniard's rapier. The first and second cause will not serve my turn; the passado he respects not, the duello he regards not. His disgrace is to be called boy, but 180 his glory is to subdue men. Adieu, valour! rust, rapier! be still, drum! for your manager is in love; yea, he loveth. Assist me, some extemporal god of rhyme, for I am sure I shall turn sonnet. Devise, wit! write, pen! for I am for whole volumes in folio.

[*Exit.*

IN THE PARK

ACT II

SCENE I. *The Park. A Pavilion and Tents at a Distance*

Enter the PRINCESS OF FRANCE, ROSALINE, MARIA, KATHERINE, BOYET, Lords, *and other* Attendants

Boyet. Now, madam, summon up your dearest spirits.
Consider who the king your father sends,
To whom he sends, and what 's his embassy:
Yourself, held precious in the world's esteem,
To parley with the sole inheritor
Of all perfections that a man may owe,
Matchless Navarre; the plea of no less weight
Than Aquitaine, a dowry for a queen.
Be now as prodigal of all dear grace

As Nature was in making graces dear   10
When she did starve the general world beside
And prodigally gave them all to you.

    Princess. Good Lord Boyet, my beauty, though but
        mean,
Needs not the painted flourish of your praise ;
Beauty is bought by judgment of the eye,
Not utter'd by base sale of chapmen's tongues.
I am less proud to hear you tell my worth
Than you much willing to be counted wise
In spending your wit in the praise of mine.
But now to task the tasker : good Boyet,   20
You are not ignorant, all-telling fame
Doth noise abroad, Navarre hath made a vow,
Till painful study shall outwear three years,
No woman may approach his silent court.
Therefore to 's seemeth it a needful course,
Before we enter his forbidden gates,
To know his pleasure ; and in that behalf,
Bold of your worthiness, we single you
As our best-moving fair solicitor.
Tell him the daughter of the King of France,   30
On serious business, craving quick dispatch,
Importunes personal conference with his grace.
Haste, signify so much, while we attend,
Like humble-visag'd suitors, his high will.

    Boyet. Proud of employment, willingly I go.

    Princess. All pride is willing pride, and yours is so. —

                                   [*Exit Boyet.*

Who are the votaries, my loving lords,
That are vow-fellows with this virtuous duke?

   1 *Lord.* Lord Longaville is one.

   Princess.   Know you the man?

   Maria. I know him, madam; at a marriage-feast, 40
Between Lord Perigort and the beauteous heir
Of Jaques Falconbridge, solemnized
In Normandy, saw I this Longaville.
A man of sovereign parts he is esteem'd,
Well fitted in the arts, glorious in arms;
Nothing becomes him ill that he would well.
The only soil of his fair virtue's gloss —
If virtue's gloss will stain with any soil —
Is a sharp wit match'd with too blunt a will,
Whose edge hath power to cut, whose will still wills 50
It should none spare that come within his power.

   Princess. Some merry mocking lord, belike; is 't so?

   Maria. They say so most that most his humours
      know.

   Princess. Such short-liv'd wits do wither as they
      grow.
Who are the rest?

   Katherine. The young Dumain, a well-accomplish'd
      youth,
Of all that virtue love for virtue lov'd;
Most power to do most harm, least knowing ill,
For he hath wit to make an ill shape good,
And shape to win grace though he had no wit. 60
I saw him at the Duke Alençon's once;

And much too little of that good I saw
Is my report to his great worthiness.

  Rosaline. Another of these students at that time
Was there with him, if I have heard a truth.
Biron they call him; but a merrier man,
Within the limit of becoming mirth,
I never spent an hour's talk withal.
His eye begets occasion for his wit;
For every object that the one doth catch   70
The other turns to a mirth-moving jest,
Which his fair tongue, conceit's expositor,
Delivers in such apt and gracious words
That aged ears play truant at his tales
And younger hearings are quite ravished,
So sweet and voluble is his discourse.

  Princess. God bless my ladies! are they all in love,
That every one her own hath garnished
With such bedecking ornaments of praise?

  1 *Lord.* Here comes Boyet.

Re-enter BOYET

  Princess.   Now, what admittance, lord?
  Boyet. Navarre had notice of your fair approach, 81
And he and his competitors in oath
Were all address'd to meet you, gentle lady,
Before I came.   Marry, thus much I have learnt:
He rather means to lodge you in the field,
Like one that comes here to besiege his court,
Than seek a dispensation for his oath,

To let you enter his unpeopled house. —
Here comes Navarre.

Enter KING, LONGAVILLE, DUMAIN, BIRON, *and*
Attendants

 King. Fair princess, welcome to the court of Navarre. 90
 Princess. Fair I give you back again, and welcome
I have not yet; the roof of this court is too high to
be yours, and welcome to the wide fields too base to
be mine.
 King. You shall be welcome, madam, to my court.
 Princess. I will be welcome, then; conduct me
  thither.
 King. Hear me, dear lady; I have sworn an oath.
 Princess. Our Lady help my lord! he 'll be forsworn.
 King. Not for the world, fair madam, by my will.
 Princess. Why, will shall break it, will and nothing
  else.   100
 King. Your ladyship is ignorant what it is.
 Princess. Were my lord so, his ignorance were wise,
Where now his knowledge must prove ignorance.
I hear your grace hath sworn out house-keeping;
'T is deadly sin to keep that oath, my lord,
And sin to break it.
But pardon me, I am too sudden-bold;
To teach a teacher ill beseemeth me.
Vouchsafe to read the purpose of my coming,
And suddenly resolve me in my suit.   110
 King. Madam, I will, if suddenly I may.

Princess. You will the sooner that I were away,
For you'll prove perjur'd if you make me stay.

Biron. Did not I dance with you in Brabant once?

Rosaline. Did not I dance with you in Brabant once?

Biron. I know you did.

Rosaline. How needless was it then to ask the question!

Biron. You must not be so quick.

Rosaline. 'T is long of you that spur me with such questions.

Biron. Your wit's too hot, it speeds too fast, 't will tire.   120

Rosaline. Not till it leave the rider in the mire.

Biron. What time o' day?

Rosaline. The hour that fools should ask.

Biron. Now fair befall your mask!

Rosaline. Fair fall the face it covers!

Biron. And send you many lovers!

Rosaline. Amen, so you be none.

Biron. Nay, then will I be gone.

King. Madam, your father here doth intimate
The payment of a hundred thousand crowns;   130
Being but the one half of an entire sum
Disbursed by my father in his wars.
But say that he or we, as neither have,
Receiv'd that sum, yet there remains unpaid
A hundred thousand more, in surety of the which
One part of Aquitaine is bound to us,
Although not valued to the money's worth.

If then the king your father will restore
But that one half which is unsatisfied,
We will give up our right in Aquitaine,   140
And hold fair friendship with his majesty.
But that, it seems, he little purposeth,
For here he doth demand to have repaid
A hundred thousand crowns ; and not demands,
On payment of a hundred thousand crowns,
To have his title live in Aquitaine,
Which we much rather had depart withal,
And have the money by our father lent,
Than Aquitaine so gelded as it is.
Dear princess, were not his requests so far   150
From reason's yielding, your fair self should make
A yielding 'gainst some reason in my breast,
And go well satisfied to France again.

    Princess. You do the king my father too much wrong,
And wrong the reputation of your name,
In so unseeming to confess receipt
Of that which hath so faithfully been paid.

    King. I do protest I never heard of it ;
And if you prove it, I 'll repay it back
Or yield up Aquitaine.

    Princess.   We arrest your word. —   160
Boyet, you can produce acquittances
For such a sum from special officers
Of Charles his father.

    King.   Satisfy me so.

    Boyet. So please your grace, the packet is not come

Where that and other specialties are bound;
To-morrow you shall have a sight of them.

   King. It shall suffice me; at which interview
All liberal reason I will yield unto.
Meantime receive such welcome at my hand
As honour without breach of honour may   170
Make tender of to thy true worthiness.
You may not come, fair princess, in my gates;
But here without you shall be so receiv'd
As you shall deem yourself lodg'd in my heart,
Though so denied fair harbour in my house.
Your own good thoughts excuse me, and farewell;
To-morrow shall we visit you again.

   Princess. Sweet health and fair desires consort your
      grace!

   King. Thy own wish wish I thee in every place!

                                   [*Exit.*

   Biron. Lady, I will commend you to mine own
heart.   180

   Rosaline. Pray you, do my commendations; I
would be glad to see it.

   Biron. I would you heard it groan.

   Rosaline. Is the fool sick?

   Biron. Sick at the heart.

   Rosaline. Alack, let it blood.

   Biron. Would that do it good?

   Rosaline. My physic says ay.

   Biron. Will you prick 't with your eye?

   Rosaline. No point, with my knife.   190

Biron. Now, God save thy life !

Rosaline. And yours from long living !

Biron. I cannot stay thanksgiving.   [*Retiring.*

Dumain. Sir, I pray you, a word : what lady is that same ?

Boyet. The heir of Alençon, Katherine her name.

Dumain. A gallant lady. Monsieur, fare you well.

[*Exit.*

Longaville. I beseech you a word : what is she in the white ?

Boyet. A woman sometimes, an you saw her in the light.

Longaville. Perchance light in the light. I desire her name.

Boyet. She hath but one for herself ; to desire that were a shame.   200

Longaville. Pray you, sir, whose daughter ?

Boyet. Her mother's, I have heard.

Longaville. God's blessing on your beard !

Boyet. Good sir, be not offended.

She is an heir of Falconbridge.

Longaville. Nay, my choler is ended.

She is a most sweet lady.

Boyet. Not unlike, sir, that may be.

[*Exit Longaville.*

Biron. What 's her name in the cap ?

Boyet. Rosaline, by good hap.   210

Biron. Is she wedded or no ?

Boyet. To her will, sir, or so.

Biron. You are welcome, sir ; adieu.

Boyet. Farewell to me, sir, and welcome to you.

[*Exit Biron.*

Maria. That last is Biron, the merry mad-cap lord ;
Not a word with him but a jest.

Boyet.   And every jest but a word.

Princess. It was well done of you to take him at his
    word.

Boyet. I was as willing to grapple as he was to board.

Maria. Two hot sheeps, marry.

Boyet.   And wherefore not ships ?
No sheep, sweet lamb, unless we feed on your lips.   220

Maria. You sheep, and I pasture ; shall that finish
    the jest ?

Boyet. So you grant pasture for me.

[*Offering to kiss her.*

Maria.   Not so, gentle beast ;
My lips are no common, though several they be.

Boyet. Belonging to whom ?

Maria.   To my fortunes and me.

Princess. Good wits will be jangling ; but, gentles,
    agree.
This civil war of wits were much better us'd
On Navarre and his book-men, for here 't is abus'd.

Boyet. If my observation, which very seldom lies,
By the heart's still rhetoric disclosed with eyes,
Deceive me not now, Navarre is infected.   230

Princess. With what ?

Boyet. With that which we lovers entitle affected.

Princess. Your reason?

Boyet. Why, all his behaviours did make their retire
To the court of his eye, peeping thorough desire;
His heart, like an agate, with your print impress'd,
Proud with his form, in his eye pride express'd;
His tongue, all impatient to speak and not see,
Did stumble with haste in his eyesight to be;
All senses to that sense did make their repair,   240
To feel only looking on fairest of fair.
Methought all his senses were lock'd in his eye,
As jewels in crystal for some prince to buy,
Who, tendering their own worth from where they were
        glass'd,
Did point you to buy them, along as you pass'd.
His face's own margent did quote such amazes
That all eyes saw his eyes enchanted with gazes.
I'll give you Aquitaine and all that is his,
An you give him for my sake but one loving kiss.

Princess. Come to our pavilion; Boyet is dispos'd. 250

Boyet. But to speak that in words which his eye hath
        disclos'd.
I only have made a mouth of his eye
By adding a tongue which I know will not lie.

Rosaline. Thou art an old love-monger and speakest
        skilfully.

Maria. He is Cupid's grandfather and learns news
        of him.

Rosaline. Then was Venus like her mother, for her
        father is but grim.

Boyet. Do you hear, my mad wenches?
Maria.   No.
Boyet.   What then, do you see?
Rosaline. Ay, our way to be gone.
Boyet.   You are too hard for me.
                                      [*Exeunt.*

BIRON AND COSTARD

ACT III

SCENE I. *The Park*

Enter ARMADO *and* MOTH

Armado. Warble, child; make passionate my sense of hearing.

MOTH *sings.* — *Concolinel*

Armado. Sweet air! — Go, tenderness of years; take this key, give enlargement to the swain, bring him festinately hither.   I must employ him in a letter to my love.

Moth. Master, will you win your love with a French brawl?

Armado. How meanest thou? brawling in French?

Moth. No, my complete master; but to jig off a tune at the tongue's end, canary to it with your feet,

humour it with turning up your eye, sigh a note and
sing a note, sometime through the throat, as if you
swallowed love with singing love, sometime through
the nose, as if you snuffed up love by smelling love;
with your hat penthouse-like o'er the shop of your
eyes; with your arms crossed on your thin-belly
doublet like a rabbit on a spit, or your hands in
your pocket like a man after the old painting; and
keep not too long in one tune, but a snip and away. 20
These are complements, these are humours; these
betray nice wenches, that would be betrayed without
these, and make them men of note — do you note
me? — that most are affected to these.   24

Armado. How hast thou purchased this experience?

Moth. By my penny of observation.

Armado. But O, — but O, —

Moth. The hobby-horse is forgot.

Armado. Callest thou my love hobby-horse?   30

Moth. No, master; the hobby-horse is but a colt,
and your love perhaps a hackney. But have you
forgot your love?

Armado. Almost I had.

Moth. Negligent student! learn her by heart.

Armado. By heart and in heart, boy.

Moth. And out of heart, master; all those three I
will prove.

Armado. What wilt thou prove?   39

Moth. A man, if I live; and this, by, in, and with-

out, upon the instant. By heart you love her, because your heart cannot come by her; in heart you
love her, because your heart is in love with her; and
out of heart you love her, being out of heart that you
cannot enjoy her.

Armado. I am all these three.

Moth. And three times as much more, and yet
nothing at all.

Armado. Fetch hither the swain; he must carry
me a letter.   50

Moth. A message well sympathized; a horse to
be ambassador for an ass.

Armado. Ha, ha! what sayest thou?

Moth. Marry, sir, you must send the ass upon the
horse, for he is very slow-gaited. But I go.

Armado. The way is but short; away!

Moth. As swift as lead, sir.

Armado. Thy meaning, pretty ingenious?
Is not lead a metal heavy, dull, and slow?   59

Moth. Minime, honest master; or rather, master, no.

Armado. I say lead is slow.

Moth.   You are too swift, sir, to say so;
Is that lead slow which is fir'd from a gun?

Armado. Sweet smoke of rhetoric!
He reputes me a cannon; and the bullet, that 's he. —
I shoot thee at the swain.

Moth.   Thump then, and I flee.   [*Exit.*

Armado. A most acute juvenal, voluble and free of
        grace!

By thy favour, sweet welkin, I must sigh in thy
       face. —
Most rude melancholy, valour gives thee place. —
My herald is return'd.

Re-enter MOTH with COSTARD

  Moth. A wonder, master! here's a costard broken
     in a shin.   70
  Armado. Some enigma, some riddle. Come, thy
     l'envoy; begin.
  Costard. No egma, no riddle, no l'envoy; no
salve in them all, sir. O, sir, plantain, a plain
plantain! no l'envoy, no l'envoy; no salve, sir,
but a plantain!
  Armado. By virtue, thou enforcest laughter; thy
silly thought my spleen; the heaving of my lungs
provokes me to ridiculous smiling. — O, pardon me,
my stars! Doth the inconsiderate take salve for
l'envoy, and the word l'envoy for a salve?   80
  Moth. Do the wise think them other? is not
l'envoy a salve?
  Armado. No, page; it is an epilogue or discourse, to
     make plain
Some obscure precedence that hath tofore been sain.
I will example it:
         The fox, the ape, and the humble-bee,
         Were still at odds, being but three.
There's the moral. Now the l'envoy.
  Moth. I will add the l'envoy. Say the moral again.

Armado. The fox, the ape, the humble-bee,   90
        Were still at odds, being but three.
Moth.   Until the goose came out of door,
        And stay'd the odds by adding four.

Now will I begin your moral, and do you follow with
my l'envoy.

        The fox, the ape, and the humble-bee,
        Were still at odds, being but three.

Armado. Until the goose came out of door,
        Staying the odds by adding four.

Moth. A good l'envoy, ending in the goose; would
you desire more?   101

Costard. The boy hath sold him a bargain, a goose,
    that's flat. —

Sir, your pennyworth is good, an your goose be fat. —
To sell a bargain well is as cunning as fast and
    loose.

Let me see — a fat l'envoy; ay, that's a fat goose.

Armado. Come hither, come hither. How did this
    argument begin?

Moth. By saying that a costard was broken in a
    shin.

Then call'd you for the l'envoy.

Costard. True, and I for a plantain; thus came your
    argument in,

Then the boy's fat l'envoy, the goose that you bought,
And he ended the market.   111

Armado. But tell me; how was there a costard
broken in a shin?

Moth. I will tell you sensibly.

Costard. Thou hast no feeling of it, Moth; I will speak that l'envoy.

  I Costard, running out, that was safely within,
  Fell over the threshold and broke my shin.

Armado. We will talk no more of this matter.

Costard. Till there be more matter in the shin.   120

Armado. Marry, Costard, I will enfranchise thee.

Costard. O, marry me to one Frances? I smell some l'envoy, some goose, in this.

Armado. By my sweet soul, I mean setting thee at liberty, enfreedoming thy person; thou wert immured, restrained, captivated, bound.

Costard. True, true; and now you will be my purgation and let me loose.   128

Armado. I give thee thy liberty, set thee from durance, and, in lieu thereof, impose on thee nothing but this: bear this significant [*giving a letter*] to the country maid Jaquenetta. There is remuneration; for the best ward of mine honour is rewarding my dependents. — Moth, follow.   [*Exit.*

Moth. Like the sequel, I. — Signior Costard, adieu.

Costard. My sweet ounce of man's flesh! my incony Jew! —   [*Exit Moth.*

Now will I look to his remuneration. Remuneration! O, that's the Latin word for three farthings; three farthings — remuneration. — 'What's the price of this inkle?' — 'One penny.' — 'No, I'll give you a remuneration;' why, it carries it. — Remuneration!

why, it is a fairer name than French crown. I will
never buy and sell out of this word.   143

Enter BIRON

Biron. O, my good knave Costard! exceedingly
well met.

Costard. Pray you, sir, how much carnation rib-
bon may a man buy for a remuneration?

Biron. What is a remuneration?

Costard. Marry, sir, halfpenny farthing.

Biron. Why, then, three-farthing worth of silk.   150

Costard. I thank your worship; God be wi' you!

Biron. Stay, slave! I must employ thee;
As thou wilt win my favour, good my knave,
Do one thing for me that I shall entreat.

Costard. When would you have it done, sir?

Biron. This afternoon.

Costard. Well, I will do it, sir; fare you well.

Biron. Thou knowest not what it is.

Costard. I shall know, sir, when I have done it.

Biron. Why, villain, thou must know first.   160

Costard. I will come to your worship to-morrow
        morning.

Biron. It must be done this afternoon. Hark,
slave, it is but this:
The princess comes to hunt here in the park,
And in her train there is a gentle lady;
When tongues speak sweetly, then they name her name,
And Rosaline they call her. Ask for her,

And to her white hand see thou do commend
This seal'd-up counsel. There's thy guerdon; go.   169
                              [*Giving him a shilling.*

  Costard. Gardon. — O sweet gardon! better than
remuneration, a 'leven-pence farthing better; most
sweet gardon! — I will do it, sir, in print. — Gardon!
Remuneration!   [*Exit.*

  Biron. And I, forsooth, in love! I that have
been love's whip;
A very beadle to a humorous sigh;
A critic, nay, a night-watch constable;
A domineering pedant o'er the boy
Than whom no mortal so magnificent!
This wimpled, whining, purblind, wayward boy;   180
This senior-junior, giant-dwarf, Dan Cupid;
Regent of love-rhymes, lord of folded arms,
The anointed sovereign of sighs and groans,
Liege of all loiterers and malcontents,
Dread prince of plackets, king of codpieces,
Sole imperator and great general
Of trotting paritors, — O my little heart! —
And I to be a corporal of his field,
And wear his colours like a tumbler's hoop!
What, I! I love! I sue! I seek a wife!   190
A woman, that is like a German clock,
Still a-repairing, ever out of frame,
And never going right, being a watch,
But being watch'd that it may still go right!
Nay, to be perjur'd, which is worst of all;

And, among three, to love the worst of all;
A wightly wanton with a velvet brow,
With two pitch-balls stuck in her face for eyes;
Ay, and, by heaven, one that will do the deed,
Though Argus were her eunuch and her guard!   200
And I to sigh for her! to watch for her!
To pray for her!   Go to; it is a plague
That Cupid will impose for my neglect
Of his almighty dreadful little might.
Well, I will love, write, sigh, pray, sue, and groan;
Some men must love my lady and some Joan.   [*Exit.*

ARMADO AND MOTH

ACT IV

SCENE I. *The Park*

Enter the PRINCESS, *and her train, a* FORESTER, BOYET,
ROSALINE, MARIA, *and* KATHERINE

Princess. Was that the king, that spurr'd his horse
    so hard
Against the steep uprising of the hill?
    Boyet. I know not; but I think it was not he.

Princess. Whoe'er he was, he show'd a mounting mind.
Well, lords, to-day we shall have our dispatch;
On Saturday we will return to France. —
Then, forester, my friend, where is the bush
That we must stand and play the murtherer in?

Forester. Hereby, upon the edge of yonder coppice;
A stand where you may make the fairest shoot.   10

Princess. I thank my beauty, I am fair that shoot,
And thereupon thou speak'st the fairest shoot.

Forester. Pardon me, madam, for I meant not so.

Princess. What, what? first praise me and again say no?
O short-liv'd pride! Not fair? alack for woe!

Forester. Yes, madam, fair.

Princess.   Nay, never paint me now;
Where fair is not, praise cannot mend the brow.
Here, good my glass, take this for telling true;
Fair payment for foul words is more than due.

Forester. Nothing but fair is that which you inherit.   20

Princess. See, see, my beauty will be sav'd by merit!
O heresy in fair, fit for these days!
A giving hand, though foul, shall have fair praise. —
But come, the bow; now mercy goes to kill,
And shooting well is then accounted ill.
Thus will I save my credit in the shoot:
Not wounding, pity would not let me do 't;
If wounding, then it was to show my skill,
That more for praise than purpose meant to kill.

And out of question so it is sometimes,   30
Glory grows guilty of detested crimes,
When, for fame's sake, for praise, an outward part,
We bend to that the working of the heart;
As I for praise alone now seek to spill
The poor deer's blood that my heart means no ill.

Boyet. Do not curst wives hold that self-sovereignty
Only for praise sake, when they strive to be
Lords o'er their lords?

Princess. Only for praise; and praise we may afford
To any lady that subdues a lord.   40

Boyet. Here comes a member of the commonwealth.

Enter COSTARD

Costard. God dig-you-den all! Pray you, which
is the head lady?

Princess. Thou shalt know her, fellow, by the rest
that have no heads.

Costard. Which is the greatest lady, the highest?

Princess. The thickest and the tallest.

Costard. The thickest and the tallest! it is so; truth
is truth.
An your waist, mistress, were as slender as my wit,
One o' these maids' girdles for your waist should be fit. 50
Are not you the chief woman? you are the thickest
here.

Princess. What's your will, sir? what's your will?

Costard. I have a letter from Monsieur Biron to
one Lady Rosaline.

Princess. O, thy letter, thy letter! he's a good
    friend of mine.
Stand aside, good bearer. — Boyet, you can carve;
Break up this capon.

    Boyet.   I am bound to serve. —
This letter is mistook, it importeth none here;
It is writ to Jaquenetta.

    Princess.   We will read it, I swear.
Break the neck of the wax, and every one give ear.   59

    Boyet. [Reads] '*By heaven, that thou art fair, is
most infallible; true, that thou art beauteous; truth
itself, that thou art lovely. More fairer than fair,
beautiful than beauteous, truer than truth itself, have
commiseration on thy heroical vassal! The magnani-
mous and most illustrate king Cophetua set eye upon
the pernicious and indubitate beggar Zenelophon; and
he it was that might rightly say, Veni, vidi, vici; which
to annothanize in the vulgar, — O base and obscure
vulgar! — videlicet, He came, saw, and overcame: he
came, one; saw, two; overcame, three. Who came?* 70
*the king. Why did he come? to see. Why did he see?
to overcome. To whom came he? to the beggar. What
saw he? the beggar. Who overcame he? the beggar.
The conclusion is victory. On whose side? the king's.
The captive is enriched. On whose side? the beggar's. The catastrophe is a nuptial. On whose side?
the king's. No, on both in one, or one in both. I am
the king, for so stands the comparison; thou the
beggar, for so witnesseth thy lowliness. Shall I com-*

mand thy love? I may. Shall I enforce thy love? I 80
could. Shall I entreat thy love? I will. What shalt
thou exchange for rags? robes; for tittles? titles; for
thyself? me. Thus, expecting thy reply, I profane my
lips on thy foot, my eyes on thy picture, and my heart
on thy every part. Thine, in the dearest design of
industry,   Don Adriano de Armado.

'*Thus dost thou hear the Nemean lion roar*
  '*Gainst thee, thou lamb, that standest as his prey.*
  Submissive fall his princely feet before,
    And he from forage will incline to play;   90
  But if thou strive, poor soul, what art thou then?
  Food for his rage, repasture for his den.'

Princess. What plume of feathers is he that indited
  this letter?
What vane? what weathercock? did you ever hear
  better?

Boyet. I am much deceiv'd but I remember the
  style.

Princess. Else your memory is bad, going o'er it erewhile.

Boyet. This Armado is a Spaniard that keeps here
  in court;
A phantasime, a Monarcho, and one that makes sport
To the prince and his bookmates.

Princess.   Thou fellow, a word;
Who gave thee this letter?

Costard.   I told you; my lord.   100

Princess. To whom shouldst thou give it?

Costard.   From my lord to my lady.

Princess. From which lord to which lady?

Costard. From my lord Biron, a good master of mine,

To a lady of France that he called Rosaline.

Princess. Thou hast mistaken his letter. — Come, lords, away. —

[*To Rosaline*] Here, sweet, put up this; 't will be thine another day.   [*Exeunt Princess and train.*

Boyet. Who is the suitor? who is the suitor?

Rosaline.   Shall I teach you to know?

Boyet. Ay, my continent of beauty.

Rosaline.   Why, she that bears the bow.

Finely put off!

Boyet. My lady goes to kill horns; but, if thou marry,

Hang me by the neck if horns that year miscarry.   111

Finely put on!

Rosaline. Well, then, I am the shooter.

Boyet.   And who is your deer?

Rosaline. If we choose by the horns, yourself come not near.

Finely put on, indeed!

Maria. You still wrangle with her, Boyet, and she strikes at the brow.

Boyet. But she herself is hit lower. Have I hit her now?

Rosaline. Shall I come upon thee with an old saying, that was a man when King Pepin of France was a little boy, as touching the 'hit it'?   120

Boyet. So I may answer thee with one as old, that was a woman when Queen Guinever of Britain was a little wench, as touching the 'hit it.'

Rosaline.   *Thou canst not hit it, hit it, hit it,*
                   Thou canst not hit it, my good man.

Boyet.   *An I cannot, cannot, cannot,*
                   An I cannot, another can.

                                   [*Exit Rosaline and Katherine.*

Costard. By my troth, most pleasant! how both did fit it!

Maria. A mark marvellous well shot, for they both did hit it.

Boyet. A mark! O, mark but that mark! A mark, says my lady! 130
Let the mark have a prick in 't, to mete at, if it may be.

Maria. Wide o' the bow-hand! i' faith, your hand is out.

Costard. Indeed, a' must shoot nearer, or he'll ne'er hit the clout.

Boyet. An if my hand be out, then belike your hand is in.

Costard. Then will she get the upshoot by cleaving the pin.

Maria. Come, come, you talk greasily; your lips grow foul.

Costard. She 's too hard for you at pricks, sir; challenge her to bowl.

Boyet. I fear too much rubbing.— Good-night, my good owl.   [*Exeunt Boyet and Maria.*

Costard. By my soul, a swain! a most simple
　　clown! 139

Lord, Lord, how the ladies and I have put him down!—

O' my troth, most sweet jests! most incony vulgar
　　wit!

When it comes so smoothly off, so obscenely, as it
　　were, so fit.

Armado o' th' one side,— O, a most dainty man!

To see him walk before a lady and to bear her fan!

To see him kiss his hand! and how most sweetly a'
　　will swear!

And his page o' t' other side, that handful of wit!

Ah, heavens, it is a most pathetical nit!—

Sola, sola! [*Shout within.*
　　　　　　　　　　　　　　　　　[*Exit Costard, running.*

SCENE II. *The Same*

Enter HOLOFERNES, SIR NATHANIEL, *and* DULL

Nathaniel. Very reverend sport, truly; and done
in the testimony of a good conscience.

Holofernes. The deer was, as you know, sanguis,
in blood; ripe as the pomewater, who now hangeth
like a jewel in the ear of caelo, the sky, the welkin,
the heaven, and anon falleth like a crab on the face
of terra, the soil, the land, the earth.

Nathaniel. Truly, Master Holofernes, the epithets
are sweetly varied, like a scholar at the least; but,
sir, I assure ye, it was a buck of the first head. 10

Holofernes. Sir Nathaniel, haud credo.

Dull. 'T was not a haud credo; 't was a pricket.

Holofernes. Most barbarous intimation! yet a kind of insinuation, as it were, in via, in way, of explication; facere, as it were, replication, or rather, ostentare, to show, as it were, his inclination, — after his undressed, unpolished, uneducated, unpruned, untrained, or rather, unlettered, or ratherest, unconfirmed fashion, — to insert again my haud credo for a deer.   20

Dull. I said the deer was not a haud credo; 't was a pricket.

Holofernes. Twice-sod simplicity, bis coctus! — O thou monster Ignorance, how deformed dost thou look!

Nathaniel. Sir, he hath never fed of the dainties that are bred in a book;

he hath not eat paper, as it were; he hath not drunk ink: his intellect is not replenished. He is only an animal, only sensible in the duller parts;

And such barren plants are set before us, that we thankful should be,

Which we of taste and feeling are, for those parts that do fructify in us more than he.

For as it would ill become me to be vain, indiscreet, or a fool,   30

So were there a patch set on learning, to see him in a school.

But omne bene, say I; being of an old father's mind,

Many can brook the weather that love not the wind.

Dull. You two are book-men; can you tell me by
        your wit
What was a month old at Cain's birth, that's not five
        weeks old as yet?

Holofernes. Dictynna, goodman Dull; Dictynna, good
        man Dull.

Dull. What is Dictynna?

Nathaniel. A title to Phœbe, to Luna, to the moon.

Holofernes. The moon was a month old when Adam
        was no more,
And raught not to five weeks when he came to five-
        score.   40
The allusion holds in the exchange.

Dull. 'T is true indeed; the collusion holds in the
        exchange.

Holofernes. God comfort thy capacity! I say, the
allusion holds in the exchange.

Dull. And I say, the pollution holds in the exchange, for the moon is never but a month old;
and I say beside that, 't was a pricket that the princess killed.

Holofernes. Sir Nathaniel, will you hear an extemporal epitaph on the death of the deer? And, to
humour the ignorant, call I the deer the princess
killed a pricket.   52

Nathaniel. Perge, good Master Holofernes, perge,
so it shall please you to abrogate scurrility.

Holofernes. I will something affect the letter, for
it argues facility.

The preyful princess pierc'd and prick'd a pretty pleasing
          pricket;
   Some say a sore, but not a sore till now made sore
          with shooting.
The dogs did yell; put L *to sore, then sorel jumps from*
          thicket,
   Or pricket sore, or else sorel; the people fall a-hoot-
          ing.   60
If sore be sore, then L *to sore makes fifty sores,—* O
          sore L *!*
Of one sore I an hundred make by adding but one
          more L*.*

Nathaniel. A rare talent.

Dull. [Aside] If a talent be a claw, look how he
claws him with a talent.

Holofernes. This is a gift that I have, simple,
simple; a foolish extravagant spirit, full of forms,
figures, shapes, objects, ideas, apprehensions, mo-
tions, revolutions. These are begot in the ventricle
of memory, nourished in the womb of pia mater, and
delivered upon the mellowing of occasion. But the
gift is good in those in whom it is acute, and I am
thankful for it.   73

Nathaniel. Sir, I praise the Lord for you; and so
may my parishioners, for their sons are well tutored
by you, and their daughters profit very greatly under
you. You are a good member of the commonwealth.

Holofernes. Mehercle, if their sons be ingenuous,
they shall want no instruction; if their daughters be

capable, I will put it to them.　But vir sapit qui
pauca loquitur; a soul feminine saluteth us.　　　81

Enter JAQUENETTA *and* COSTARD

Jaquenetta.　God give you good morrow, master
Person.

Holofernes.　Master Person, quasi pers-on.　An if
one should be pierced, which is the one?

Costard.　Marry, master schoolmaster, he that is
likest to a hogshead.

Holofernes.　Piercing a hogshead! a good lustre of
conceit in a turf of earth; fire enough for a flint,
pearl enough for a swine.　'T is pretty; it is well.　　90

Jaquenetta.　Good master Person, be so good as
read me this letter.　It was given me by Costard,
and sent me from Don Armado; I beseech you,
read it.

Holofernes.　Fauste, precor gelida quando pecus
omne sub umbra Ruminat, — and so forth.　Ah,
good old Mantuan! I may speak of thee as the
traveller doth of Venice:

　　　　　Venetia, Venetia,
　　　　　Chi non ti vede non ti pretia.　　100

Old Mantuan, old Mantuan! who understandeth thee
not loves thee not.　Ut, re, sol, la, mi, fa.　Under
pardon, sir, what are the contents? or rather, as
Horace says in his — What, my soul, verses?

Nathaniel.　Ay, sir, and very learned.

Holofernes. Let me hear a staff, a stanza, a verse;
lege, domine.

Nathaniel. [Reads]

' *If love make me forsworn, how shall I swear to love ?*
  Ah, never faith could hold, if not to beauty vow'd !
Though to myself forsworn, to thee I'll faithful prove ;
    Those thoughts to me were oaks, to thee like osiers
      bow'd.   111
Study his bias leaves and makes his book thine eyes,
    Where all those pleasures live that art would compre-
      hend ;
If knowledge be the mark, to know thee shall suffice.
    Well learned is that tongue that well can thee com-
      mend,
All ignorant that soul that sees thee without wonder,
    Which is to me some praise that I thy parts admire.
Thy eye Jove's lightning bears, thy voice his dreadful
      thunder,
    Which, not to anger bent, is music and sweet fire.
Celestial as thou art, O, pardon love this wrong,   120
That sings heaven's praise with such an earthly tongue.'

Holofernes. You find not the apostrophas, and so
miss the accent ; let me supervise the canzonet.
Here are only numbers ratified ; but, for the ele-
gancy, facility, and golden cadence of poesy, caret.
Ovidius Naso was the man ; and why, indeed, Naso,
but for smelling out the odoriferous flowers of fancy,
the jerks of invention ? Imitari is nothing ; so doth
the hound his master, the ape his keeper, the tired

horse his rider. — But, damosella virgin, was this
directed to you?   131

Jaquenetta. Ay, sir, from one Monsieur Biron, one
of the strange queen's lords.

Holofernes. I will overglance the superscript: ' *To
the snow-white hand of the most beauteous Lady
Rosaline.*'   I will look again on the intellect of the
letter, for the nomination of the party writing to the
person written unto: ' *Your ladyship's in all desired
employment, Biron.*'   Sir Nathaniel, this Biron is
one of the votaries with the king; and here he hath
framed a letter to a sequent of the stranger queen's,
which accidentally, or by the way of progression,
hath miscarried. — Trip and go, my sweet, deliver
this paper into the royal hand of the king; it may
concern much.   Stay not thy compliment; I for-
give thy duty.   Adieu.   146

Jaquenetta. Good Costard, go with me. — Sir,
God save your life!

Costard. Have with thee, my girl.

                     [*Exeunt Costard and Jaquenetta.*

Nathaniel. Sir, you have done this in the fear
of God, very religiously; and, as a certain father
saith, —   152

Holofernes. Sir, tell not me of the father; I do
fear colourable colours.   But to return to the verses,
did they please you, Sir Nathaniel?

Nathaniel. Marvellous well for the pen.

Holofernes. I do dine to-day at the father's of a

certain pupil of mine, where, if, before repast, it shall please you to gratify the table with a grace, I will, on my privilege I have with the parents of the foresaid child or pupil, undertake your ben venuto; where I will prove those verses to be very unlearned, neither savouring of poetry, wit, nor invention. I beseech your society. 164

Nathaniel. And thank you too; for society, saith the text, is the happiness of life.

Holofernes. And, certes, the text most infallibly concludes it. — [*To Dull*] Sir, I do invite you too; you shall not say me nay; pauca verba. — Away! the gentles are at their game, and we will to our recreation.   [*Exeunt.*

SCENE III. *The Same*

Enter BIRON, *with a paper*

Biron. The king he is hunting the deer; I am coursing myself. They have pitched a toil; I am toiling in a pitch, — pitch that defiles. Defile! a foul word. Well, set thee down, Sorrow! for so they say the fool said, and so say I, and ay the fool. Well proved, wit! By the Lord, this love is as mad as Ajax! it kills sheep; it kills me, ay, a sheep. Well proved again o' my side! I will not love; if I do, hang me; i' faith, I will not. O, but her eye, — by this light, but for her eye, I would not love her; yes, for 10 her two eyes. Well, I do nothing in the world but lie, and lie in my throat. By heaven, I do love, and it hath taught me to rhyme and to be melancholy; and here is part of my rhyme, and here my melancholy. Well, she hath one o' my sonnets already. The clown bore it, the fool sent it, and the lady hath it; sweet clown, sweeter fool, sweetest lady! By the world, I would not care a pin, if the other three were in. — Here comes one with a paper; God give him grace to groan! [*Gets up into a tree.*

Enter the KING, *with a paper*

King. Ay me! 21

Biron. [*Aside*] Shot, by heaven! — Proceed, sweet Cupid; thou hast thumped him with thy bird-bolt under the left pap. — In faith, secrets!

King. [Reads]
So sweet a kiss the golden sun gives not
 To those fresh morning drops upon the rose,
As thy eye-beams when their fresh rays have smote
 The night of dew that on my cheeks down flows;
Nor shines the silver moon one half so bright
 Through the transparent bosom of the deep 30
As doth thy face through tears of mine give light.
 Thou shin'st in every tear that I do weep;
No drop but as a coach doth carry thee,
 So ridest thou triumphing in my woe.
Do but behold the tears that swell in me,
 And they thy glory through my grief will show.

But do not love thyself; then thou wilt keep
My tears for glasses, and still make me weep.
O queen of queens! how far dost thou excel,
No thought can think, nor tongue of mortal tell.   40

How shall she know my griefs? I'll drop the paper.
Sweet leaves, shade folly. — Who is he comes here?

[Steps aside.

What, Longaville! and reading! listen, ear.

Biron. Now, in thy likeness, one more fool appear!

Enter LONGAVILLE, *with a paper*

Longaville. Ay me, I am forsworn!

Biron. Why, he comes in like a perjure, wearing
papers.

King. In love, I hope; sweet fellowship in shame!

Biron. One drunkard loves another of the name.

Longaville. Am I the first that have been perjur'd
so?

Biron. I could put thee in comfort, — not by two
that I know.   50

Thou mak'st the triumviry, the corner-cap of society,
The shape of Love's Tyburn that hangs up simplicity.

Longaville. I fear these stubborn lines lack power to
move. —

O sweet Maria, empress of my love! —
These numbers will I tear, and write in prose.

Biron. O, rhymes are guards on wanton Cupid's
hose;

Disfigure not his slop.

Longaville. This same shall go. —

[*Reads*] *Did not the heavenly rhetoric of thine eye,*
  'Gainst whom the world cannot hold argument,
Persuade my heart to this false perjury? 60
  Vows for thee broke deserve not punishment.
A woman I forswore, but I will prove,
  Thou being a goddess, I forswore not thee.
My vow was earthly, thou a heavenly love;
  Thy grace being gain'd cures all disgrace in me.
Vows are but breath, and breath a vapour is;
  Then thou, fair sun, which on my earth dost shine,
Exhal'st this vapour-vow, in thee it is.
If broken then, it is no fault of mine;
If by me broke, what fool is not so wise 70
To lose an oath to win a paradise?

Biron. This is the liver-vein, which makes flesh a
    deity,
A green goose a goddess; pure, pure idolatry.
God amend us, God amend! we are much out o' the way.

Longaville. By whom shall I send this? Company!
    stay. [*Steps aside.*

Biron. All hid, all hid; an old infant play.
Like a demigod here sit I in the sky,
And wretched fools' secrets heedfully o'er-eye. —
More sacks to the mill! O heavens, I have my wish!

Enter DUMAIN, *with a paper*

Dumain transform'd! four woodcocks in a dish! 80

Dumain. O most divine Kate!

Biron. O most profane coxcomb!

Dumain. By heaven, the wonder in a mortal eye!

Biron. By earth, she is not, corporal, there you lie.

Dumain. Her amber hairs for foul hath amber quoted.

Biron. An amber-colour'd raven was well noted.

Dumain. As upright as the cedar.

Biron.   Stoop, I say;
Her shoulder is with child.

Dumain.   As fair as day.

Biron. Ay, as some days; but then no sun must shine.

Dumain. O that I had my wish!

Longaville.   And I had mine!

King. And I mine too, good Lord!   91

Biron. Amen, so I had mine! is not that a good
    word?

Dumain. I would forget her; but a fever she
Reigns in my blood and will remember'd be.

Biron. A fever in your blood! why, then incision
Would let her out in saucers; sweet misprision!

Dumain. Once more I'll read the ode that I have
    writ.

Biron. Once more I'll mark how love can vary wit.

Dumain. [Reads]

> On a day — alack the day! —
> Love, whose month is ever May,   100
> Spied a blossom passing fair
> Playing in the wanton air;
> Through the velvet leaves the wind,
> All unseen can passage find,

That the lover, sick to death,
Wish'd himself the heaven's breath.
Air, quoth he, thy cheeks may blow;
Air, would I might triumph so!
But, alack, my hand is sworn
Ne'er to pluck thee from thy thorn; 110
Vow, alack, for youth unmeet,
Youth so apt to pluck a sweet!
Do not call it sin in me
That I am forsworn for thee;
Thou for whom Jove would swear
Juno but an Ethiope were,
And deny himself for Jove,
Turning mortal for thy love.

This will I send, and something else more plain
That shall express my true love's fasting pain. 120
O, would the King, Biron, and Longaville,
Were lovers too! Ill, to example ill,
Would from my forehead wipe a perjur'd note;
For none offend where all alike do dote.

    Longaville. [*Advancing*] Dumain, thy love is far from
        charity,
That in love's grief desir'st society;
You may look pale, but I should blush, I know,
To be o'erheard and taken napping so.

    King. [*Advancing*] Come, sir, you blush; as his
        your case is such;
You chide at him, offending twice as much. 130
You do not love Maria; Longaville

Did never sonnet for her sake compile,
Nor never lay his wreathed arms athwart
His loving bosom to keep down his heart.
I have been closely shrouded in this bush
And mark'd you both, and for you both did blush.
I heard your guilty rhymes, observ'd your fashion,
Saw sighs reek from you, noted well your pas-
  sion :
Ay me! says one ; O Jove! the other cries ;
One, her hairs were gold, crystal the other's eyes. — 140
[*To Longaville*] You would for paradise break faith
  and troth ; —
[*To Dumain*] And Jove, for your love, would infringe
  an oath.
What will Biron say when that he shall hear
Faith so infringed, which such zeal did swear ?
How will he scorn ! how will he spend his wit !
How will he triumph, leap, and laugh at it !
For all the wealth that ever I did see,
I would not have him know so much by me.
 Biron. Now step I forth to whip hypocrisy. —
             [*Advancing.*
Ah, good my liege, I pray thee, pardon me ! 150
Good heart, what grace hast thou, thus to reprove
These worms for loving, that art most in love ?
Your eyes do make no coaches ; in your tears
There is no certain princess that appears ;
You 'll not be perjur'd, 't is a hateful thing ;
Tush, none but minstrels like of sonneting !

But are you not asham'd? nay, are you not,
All three of you, to be thus much o'ershot?
You found his mote; the king your mote did see;
But I a beam do find in each of three.   160
O, what a scene of foolery have I seen,
Of sighs, of groans, of sorrow, and of teen!
O me, with what strict patience have I sat,
To see a king transformed to a gnat!
To see great Hercules whipping a gig,
And profound Solomon to tune a jig,
And Nestor play at push-pin with the boys,
And critic Timon laugh at idle toys!—
Where lies thy grief, O, tell me, good Dumain?—
And, gentle Longaville, where lies thy pain?—   170
And where my liege's? all about the breast.—
A caudle, ho!

   King.   Too bitter is thy jest.
Are we betray'd thus to thy over-view?

   Biron. Not you to me, but I betray'd by you:
I, that am honest; I, that hold it sin
To break the vow I am engaged in;
I am betray'd, by keeping company
With men like you, men of inconstancy.
When shall you see me write a thing in rhyme?
Or groan for love? or spend a minute's time   180
In pruning me? When shall you hear that I
Will praise a hand, a foot, a face, an eye,
A gait, a state, a brow, a breast, a waist,
A leg, a limb?—

King.   Soft ! whither away so fast ?
A true man or a thief that gallops so ?
     Biron. I post from love ; good lover, let me go.

          Enter JAQUENETTA *and* COSTARD

Jaquenetta. God bless the king !
     King.   What present hast thou there ?
Costard. Some certain treason.
     King.   What makes treason here ?
Costard. Nay, it makes nothing, sir.
     King.   If it mar nothing neither,
The treason and you go in peace away together.   190
     Jaquenetta. I beseech your grace let this letter be
          read.
Our person misdoubts it ; 't was treason, he said.
     King. Biron, read it over. — [*Giving him the paper.*
Where hadst thou it ?
     Jaquenetta. Of Costard.
     King. Where hadst thou it ?
     Costard. Of Dun Adramadio, Dun Adramadio.
                    [*Biron tears the letter.*
King. How now ! what is in you ? why dost thou
          tear it ?
Biron. A toy, my liege, a toy ; your grace needs not
          fear it.
Longaville. It did move him to passion, and there-
          fore let 's hear it.   200
Dumain. It is Biron's writing, and here is his name.
                    [*Gathering up the pieces.*

Biron. [*To Costard*] Ah, you whoreson loggerhead !
 you were born to do me shame. —
Guilty, my lord, guilty ! I confess, I confess.
 King. What ?
 Biron. That you three fools lack'd me fool to make
 up the mess.
He, he, and you, and you, my liege, and I,
Are pick-purses in love, and we deserve to die.
O, dismiss this audience, and I shall tell you more.
 Dumain. Now the number is even.
 Biron.   True, true ; we are four. —
Will these turtles be gone ?
 King.   Hence, sirs ; away ! 210
 Costard. Walk aside the true folk, and let the traitors
  stay.   [*Exeunt Costard and Jaquenetta.*
 Biron. Sweet lords, sweet lovers, O, let us embrace !
 As true we are as flesh and blood can be.
The sea will ebb and flow, heaven show his face ;
 Young blood doth not obey an old decree.
We cannot cross the cause why we were born ;
Therefore of all hands must we be forsworn.
 King. What, did these rent lines show some love of
  thine ?
 Biron. Did they, quoth you ? Who sees the heavenly
  Rosaline,
That, like a rude and savage man of Inde, 220
 At the first opening of the gorgeous east,
Bows not his vassal head, and strucken blind
 Kisses the base ground with obedient breast ?

What peremptory eagle-sighted eye
  Dares look upon the heaven of her brow,
That is not blinded by her majesty?
    King. What zeal, what fury hath inspir'd thee now?
My love, her mistress, is a gracious moon;
  She an attending star, scarce seen a light.
    Biron. My eyes are then no eyes, nor I Biron.   230
  O, but for my love, day would turn to night!
Of all complexions the cull'd sovereignty
  Do meet, as at a fair, in her fair cheek,
Where several worthies make one dignity,
  Where nothing wants that want itself doth seek.
Lend me the flourish of all gentle tongues, —
  Fie, painted rhetoric! O, she needs it not!
To things of sale a seller's praise belongs,
  She passes praise; then praise too short doth blot.
A wither'd hermit, five-score winters worn,   240
  Might shake off fifty, looking in her eye;
Beauty doth varnish age, as if new-born,
  And gives the crutch the cradle's infancy.
O, 't is the sun that maketh all things shine!
    King. By heaven, thy love is black as ebony.
    Biron. Is ebony like her? O wood divine!
A wife of such wood were felicity.
O, who can give an oath? where is a book?
  That I may swear beauty doth beauty lack,
If that she learn not of her eye to look;   250
  No face is fair that is not full so black.
    King. O paradox! Black is the badge of hell,

The hue of dungeons, and the shade of night;
And beauty's crest becomes the heavens well.
 Biron. Devils soonest tempt, resembling spirits of
  light.
O, if in black my lady's brows be deck'd,
 It mourns that painting and usurping hair
Should ravish doters with a false aspect;
 And therefore is she born to make black fair.
Her favour turns the fashion of the days,   260
 For native blood is counted painting now,
And therefore red, that would avoid dispraise,
 Paints itself black, to imitate her brow.
 Dumain. To look like her are chimney-sweepers
  black.
 Longaville. And since her time are colliers counted
  bright.
 King. And Ethiopes of their sweet complexion crack.
 Dumain. Dark needs no candles now, for dark is light.
 Biron. Your mistresses dare never come in rain,
For fear their colours should be wash'd away.
 King. 'T were good yours did; for, sir, to tell you
  plain,   270
I 'll find a fairer face not wash'd to-day.
 Biron. I 'll prove her fair, or talk till doomsday here.
 King. No devil will fright thee then so much as
  she.
 Dumain. I never knew man hold vile stuff so dear.
 Longaville. Look, here 's thy love; my foot and her
  face see.

Biron. O, if the streets were paved with thine eyes,
Her feet were much too dainty for such tread !
Dumain. O vile ! then, as she goes, what upward lies
The street should see as she walk'd overhead.
King. But what of this ? are we not all in love ?   280
Biron. Nothing so sure ; and thereby all forsworn.
King. Then leave this chat ; and, good Biron, now
    prove
Our loving lawful, and our faith not torn.
Dumain. Ay, marry, there ; some flattery for this evil.
Longaville. O, some authority how to proceed ;
Some tricks, some quillets, how to cheat the devil.
Dumain. Some salve for perjury.
Biron.   'T is more than need.
Have at you, then, affection's men at arms.
Consider what you first did swear unto, —
To fast, to study, and to see no woman ;   290
Flat treason 'gainst the kingly state of youth.
Say, can you fast ? your stomachs are too young,
And abstinence engenders maladies.
And where that you have vow'd to study, lords,
In that each of you have forsworn his book,
Can you still dream and pore and thereon look ?
[For when would you, my lord, — or you, — or you, —
Have found the ground of study's excellence
Without the beauty of a woman's face ?
From women's eyes this doctrine I derive :   300
They are the ground, the books, the academes,
From whence doth spring the true Promethean fire.]

Why, universal plodding poisons up
The nimble spirits in the arteries,
As motion and long-during action tires
The sinewy vigour of the traveller.
Now, for not looking on a woman's face,
You have in that forsworn the use of eyes,
And study too, the causer of your vow ;
[For where is any author in the world   310
Teaches such beauty as a woman's eye ?
Learning is but an adjunct to ourself,
And where we are our learning likewise is ;
Then when ourselves we see in ladies' eyes,
Do we not likewise see our learning there ?
O, we have made a vow to study, lords,
And in that vow we have forsworn our books.]
For when would you, my liege, — or you, — or you, —
In leaden contemplation have found out
Such fiery numbers as the prompting eyes   320
Of beauty's tutors have enrich'd you with ?
Other slow arts entirely keep the brain,
And therefore, finding barren practisers,
Scarce show a harvest of their heavy toil ;
But love, first learned in a lady's eyes,
Lives not alone immured in the brain,
But, with the motion of all elements,
Courses as swift as thought in every power,
And gives to every power a double power,
Above their functions and their offices.   330
It adds a precious seeing to the eye ;

A lover's eyes will gaze an eagle blind ;
A lover's ear will hear the lowest sound
When the suspicious head of theft is stopp'd ;
Love's feeling is more soft and sensible
Than are the tender horns of cockled snails ;
Love's tongue proves dainty Bacchus gross in taste.
For valour, is not Love a Hercules,
Still climbing trees in the Hesperides ?
Subtle as Sphinx ; as sweet and musical   340
As bright Apollo's lute, strung with his hair ;
And when Love speaks, the voice of all the gods
Make heaven drowsy with the harmony.
Never durst poet touch a pen to write
Until his ink were temper'd with Love's sighs ;
O, then his lines would ravish savage ears
And plant in tyrants mild humility !
From women's eyes this doctrine I derive :
They sparkle still the right Promethean fire ;
They are the books, the arts, the academes,   350
That show, contain, and nourish all the world,
Else none at all in aught proves excellent.
Then fools you were these women to forswear,
Or keeping what is sworn, you will prove fools.
For wisdom's sake, a word that all men love,
Or for love's sake, a word that loves all men,
Or for men's sake, the authors of these women,
Or women's sake, by whom we men are men,
Let us once lose our oaths to find ourselves,
Or else we lose ourselves to keep our oaths.   360

It is religion to be thus forsworn,
For charity itself fulfils the law, —
And who can sever love from charity?

   King. Saint Cupid, then! and, soldiers, to the field!

   Biron. Advance your standards, and upon them,
      lords!
Pell-mell, down with them! but be first advis'd,
In conflict that you get the sun of them.

   Longaville. Now to plain-dealing; lay these glozes
      by.
Shall we resolve to woo these girls of France?

   King. And win them too; therefore let us devise
Some entertainment for them in their tents.   371

   Biron. First, from the park let us conduct them
      thither;
Then homeward every man attach the hand
Of his fair mistress. In the afternoon
We will with some strange pastime solace them,
Such as the shortness of the time can shape;
For revels, dances, masks, and merry hours
Forerun fair Love, strewing her way with flowers.

   King. Away, away! no time shall be omitted
That will be time, and may by us be fitted.   380

   Biron. Allons! allons! — Sow'd cockle reap'd no
      corn,
   And justice always whirls in equal measure.
Light wenches may prove plagues to men forsworn;
   If so, our copper buys no better treasure.   [*Exeunt.*

HOLOFERNES AND MOTH

ACT V

Scene I. *The Park*

Enter Holofernes, Sir Nathaniel, *and* Dull

Holofernes. Satis quod sufficit.

Nathaniel. I praise God for you, sir; your reasons at dinner have been sharp and sententious, pleasant without scurrility, witty without affection, audacious without impudency, learned without opinion, and strange without heresy. I did converse this quondam day with a companion of the king's, who is intituled, nominated, or called, Don Adriano de Armado.

Holofernes. Novi hominem tanquam te; his humour is lofty, his discourse peremptory, his tongue filed, his eye ambitious, his gait majestical, and his general behaviour vain, ridiculous, and thrasonical. He is too picked, too spruce, too affected, too odd, as it were, too peregrinate, as I may call it.　　　14

Nathaniel. A most singular and choice epithet.

　　　　　　　　　　　　[*Draws out his table-book.*

Holofernes. He draweth out the thread of his verbosity finer than the staple of his argument. I abhor such fanatical phantasimes, such insociable and point-device companions; such rackers of orthography, as to speak dout, fine, when he should say 20 doubt; det, when he should pronounce debt, —d, e, b, t, not d, e, t; he clepeth a calf, cauf; half, hauf; neighbour vocatur nebour; neigh abbreviated ne. This is abhominable, — which he would call abominable; it insinuateth me of insanire. Ne intelligis, domine? to make frantic, lunatic.

Nathaniel. Laus Deo, bone, intelligo.

Holofernes. Bone! — bone for bene! Priscian a little scratched; 't will serve.

Nathaniel. Videsne quis venit?　　　30

Holofernes. Video, et gaudeo.

　　　　Enter ARMADO, MOTH, *and* COSTARD

Armado. Chirrah!　　　　　　　　　　[*To Moth.*

Holofernes. Quare chirrah, not sirrah?

Armado. Men of peace, well encountered.

Holofernes. Most military sir, salutation.

Moth. [*Aside to Costard*] They have been at a great feast of languages and stolen the scraps.

Costard. O, they have lived long on the alms-basket of words. I marvel thy master hath not eaten thee for a word, for thou art not so long by the head as honorificabilitudinitatibus; thou art easier swallowed than a flap-dragon.   42

Moth. Peace! the peal begins.

Armado. [*To Holofernes*] Monsieur, are you not lettered?

Moth. Yes, yes; he teaches boys the horn-book. What is a, b, spelt backward, with the horn on his head?

Holofernes. Ba, pueritia, with a horn added.

Moth. Ba, most silly sheep with a horn! You hear his learning.   51

Holofernes. Quis, quis, thou consonant?

Moth. The third of the five vowels, if you repeat them; or the fifth, if I.

Holofernes. I will repeat them, — a, e, i, —

Moth. The sheep; the other two concludes it, — o, u.

Armado. Now, by the salt wave of the Mediter-raneum, a sweet touch, a quick venue of wit! snip, snap, quick and home! it rejoiceth my intellect; true wit!   61

Moth. Offered by a child to an old man, which is wit-old.

Holofernes. What is the figure? what is the figure?

Moth. Horns.

Holofernes. Thou disputest like an infant; go, whip thy gig.

Moth. Lend me your horn to make one, and I will whip about your infamy *circum circa,* — a gig of a cuckold's horn.   70

Costard. An I had but one penny in the world, thou shouldst have it to buy gingerbread. Hold, there is the very remuneration I had of thy master, thou halfpenny purse of wit, thou pigeon-egg of discretion. O, an the heavens were so pleased that thou wert but my bastard, what a joyful father wouldst thou make me! Go to; thou hast it *ad dunghill,* at the finger's ends, as they say.

Holofernes. O, I smell false Latin, — dunghill for *unguem!*   80

Armado. Arts-man, preambulate; we will be singled from the barbarous. Do you not educate youth at the charge-house on the top of the mountain?

Holofernes. Or *mons,* the hill.

Armado. At your sweet pleasure, for the mountain.

Holofernes. I do, sans question.

Armado. Sir, it is the king's most sweet pleasure and affection to congratulate the princess at her pavilion in the posteriors of this day, which the rude multitude call the afternoon.   90

Holofernes. The posterior of the day, most generous sir, is liable, congruent, and measurable for the afternoon; the word is well culled, choice, sweet, and apt, I do assure you, sir, I do assure.

Armado. Sir, the king is a noble gentleman, and my familiar, I do assure ye, very good friend; for what is inward between us, let it pass. I do beseech thee, remember thy courtesy, — I beseech thee, apparel thy head; — and among other importunate and most serious designs, and of great import indeed, too, — but let that pass; — for I must tell thee, it will please his grace, by the world, sometime to lean upon my poor shoulder, and with his royal finger, thus, dally with my excrement, with my mustachio, — but, sweet heart, let that pass. By the world, I recount no fable; some certain special honours it pleaseth his greatness to impart to Armado, a soldier, a man of travel, that hath seen the world, — but let that pass. — The very all of all is, — but, sweet heart, I do implore secrecy, — that the king would have me present the princess, sweet chuck, with some delightful ostentation, or show, or pageant, or antique, or firework. Now, understanding that the curate and your sweet self are good at such eruptions and sudden breaking out of mirth, as it were, I have acquainted you withal, to the end to crave your assistance.

Holofernes. Sir, you shall present before her the Nine Worthies. — Sir Nathaniel, as concerning some entertainment of time, some show in the posterior of this day, to be rendered by our assistants, at the king's command, and this most gallant, illustrate, and learned gentleman, before the princess, — I say none so fit as to present the Nine Worthies.   124

Nathaniel. Where will you find men worthy enough to present them?

Holofernes. Joshua, yourself; myself or this gallant gentleman, Judas Maccabæus; this swain, because of his great limb or joint, shall pass Pompey the Great; the page, Hercules, —   130

Armado. Pardon, sir, error; he is not quantity enough for that worthy's thumb, he is not so big as the end of his club.

Holofernes. Shall I have audience? he shall present Hercules in minority; his enter and exit shall be strangling a snake, and I will have an apology for that purpose.

Moth. An excellent device! so, if any of the audience hiss, you may cry 'Well done, Hercules! now thou crushest the snake!' that is the way to make an offence gracious, though few have the grace to do it.

Armado. For the rest of the Worthies? —   142

Holofernes. I will play three myself.

Moth. Thrice worthy gentleman!

Armado. Shall I tell you a thing?

Holofernes. We attend.

Armado. We will have, if this fadge not, an antique. I beseech you, follow.

Holofernes. Via!—Goodman Dull, thou hast
spoken no word all this while.   150

Dull. Nor understood none neither, sir.

Holofernes. Allons! we will employ thee.

Dull. I'll make one in a dance, or so; or I will
play

On the tabor to the Worthies, and let them dance
the hay.

Holofernes. Most dull, honest Dull!—To our sport,
away!   [*Exeunt.*

Scene II.   *The Same*

Enter the Princess, Katherine, Rosaline, *and* Maria

Princess. Sweet hearts, we shall be rich ere we depart

If fairings come thus plentifully in.

A lady wall'd about with diamonds!—

Look you what I have from the loving king.

Rosaline. Madame, came nothing else along with
that?

Princess. Nothing but this! yes, as much love in
rhyme

As would be cramm'd up in a sheet of paper,

Writ on both sides the leaf, margent and all,

That he was fain to seal on Cupid's name.

Rosaline. That was the way to make his godhead
wax,   10

For he hath been five thousand years a boy.

Katherine. Ay, and a shrewd, unhappy gallows too.

Rosaline. You'll ne'er be friends with him; he kill'd
your sister.

Katherine. He made her melancholy, sad, and heavy;
And so she died.   Had she been light, like you,
Of such a merry, nimble, stirring spirit,
She might ha' been a grandam ere she died;
And so may you, for a light heart lives long.

Rosaline. What's your dark meaning, mouse, of this
light word?

Katherine. A light condition in a beauty dark.   20

Rosaline. We need more light to find your meaning
out.

Katherine. You'll mar the light by taking it in snuff,
Therefore I'll darkly end the argument.

Rosaline. Look, what you do, you do it still i' the
dark.

Katherine. So do not you, for you are a light wench.

Rosaline. Indeed I weigh not you, and therefore
light.

Katherine. You weigh me not?   O, that's you care
not for me!

Rosaline. Great reason; for past cure is still past
care.

Princess. Well bandied both; a set of wit well
play'd. —
But, Rosaline, you have a favour, too.   30
Who sent it? and what is it?

Rosaline.   I would you knew.
An if my face were but as fair as yours,

My favour were as great; be witness this.
Nay, I have verses too, I thank Biron;
The numbers true, and, were the numbering too,
I were the fairest goddess on the ground.
I am compar'd to twenty thousand fairs.
O, he hath drawn my picture in his letter!

    Princess. Any thing like?

    Rosaline. Much in the letters, nothing in the praise.

    Princess. Beauteous as ink; a good conclusion.   41

    Katherine. Fair as a text B in a copy-book.

    Rosaline. Ware pencils, ho! let me not die your
        debtor,
My red dominical, my golden letter!
O that your face were not so full of O's!

    Katherine. A pox of that jest! and beshrew all
        shrows.

    Princess. But, Katherine, what was sent to you from
        fair Dumain?

    Katherine. Madam, this glove.

    Princess.   Did he not send you twain?

    Katherine. Yes, madam, and moreover
Some thousand verses of a faithful lover, —   50
A huge translation of hypocrisy,
Vilely compil'd, profound simplicity.

    Maria. This and these pearls to me sent Longaville;
The letter is too long by half a mile.

    Princess. I think no less. Dost thou not wish in
        heart
The chain were longer and the letter short?

Maria. Ay, or I would these hands might never part.

Princess. We are wise girls to mock our lovers so.

Rosaline. They are worse fools to purchase mocking so.

That same Biron I'll torture ere I go.   60

O that I knew he were but in by the week!

How I would make him fawn and beg and seek,

And wait the season, and observe the times,

And spend his prodigal wits in bootless rhymes,

And shape his service wholly to my hests,

And make him proud to make me proud that jests!

So potent-like would I o'ersway his state

That he should be my fool and I his fate.

Princess. None are so surely caught, when they are catch'd,

As wit turn'd fool; folly, in wisdom hatch'd,   70

Hath wisdom's warrant and the help of school,

And wit's own grace to grace a learned fool.

Rosaline. The blood of youth burns not with such excess

As gravity's revolt to wantonness.

Maria. Folly in fools bears not so strong a note

As foolery in the wise, when wit doth dote;

Since all the power thereof it doth apply

To prove, by wit, worth in simplicity.

Princess. Here comes Boyet, and mirth is in his face.

Enter BOYET

Boyet. O, I am stabb'd with laughter! Where 's
    her grace?   80

Princess. Thy news, Boyet?

Boyet.   Prepare, madam, prepare!—

Arm, wenches, arm! encounters mounted are

Against your peace. Love doth approach disguis'd,

Armed in arguments; you 'll be surpris'd.

Muster your wits, stand in your own defence,

Or hide your heads like cowards and fly hence.

Princess. Saint Denis to Saint Cupid! What are
    they

That charge their breath against us? say, scout, say.

Boyet. Under the cool shade of a sycamore

I thought to close mine eyes some half an hour   90

When, lo! to interrupt my purpos'd rest,

Toward that shade I might behold addrest

The king and his companions; warily

I stole into a neighbour thicket by,

And overheard what you shall overhear,—

That, by and by, disguis'd they will be here.

Their herald is a pretty knavish page,

That well by heart hath conn'd his embassage.

Action and accent did they teach him there,—

'Thus must thou speak,' and 'thus thy body bear;' 100

And ever and anon they made a doubt

Presence majestical would put him out.

For,' quoth the king, 'an angel shalt thou see;

Yet fear not thou, but speak audaciously.'
The boy replied, ' An angel is not evil ;
I should have fear'd her had she been a devil.'
With that, all laugh'd and clapp'd him on the shoulder,
Making the bold wag by their praises bolder.
One rubb'd his elbow thus, and fleer'd, and swore
A better speech was never spoke before ;   110
Another, with his finger and his thumb,
Cried, ' Via ! we will do 't, come what will come ; '
The third he caper'd, and cried, ' All goes well ; '
The fourth turn'd on the toe, and down he fell.
With that, they all did tumble on the ground,
With such a zealous laughter, so profound,
That in this spleen ridiculous appears,
To check their folly, passion's solemn tears.

   Princess.   But what, but what, come they to visit us ?

   Boyet.   They do, they do ; and are apparell'd thus,
Like Muscovites or Russians, as I guess.   121
Their purpose is to parle, to court, and dance ;
And every one his love-feat will advance
Unto his several mistress, which they 'll know
By favours several which they did bestow.

   Princess.   And will they so ? the gallants shall be task'd ;
For, ladies, we will every one be mask'd,
And not a man of them shall have the grace,
Despite of suit, to see a lady's face. —
Hold, Rosaline, this favour thou shalt wear,   130
And then the king will court thee for his dear ;
Hold, take thou this, my sweet, and give me thine,

So shall Biron take me for Rosaline. —
And change you favours too; so shall your loves
Woo contrary, deceiv'd by these removes.

    Rosaline. Come on, then; wear the favours most in
        sight.

    Katherine. But in this changing what is your intent?

    Princess. The effect of my intent is to cross theirs;
They do it but in mocking merriment,
And mock for mock is only my intent.   140
Their several counsels they unbosom shall
To loves mistook, and so be mock'd withal
Upon the next occasion that we meet,
With visages display'd, to talk and greet.

    Rosaline. But shall we dance, if they desire us to 't?

    Princess. No, to the death, we will not move a foot;
Nor to their penn'd speech render we no grace,
But while 't is spoke each turn away her face.

    Boyet. Why, that contempt will kill the speaker's
        heart,
And quite divorce his memory from his part.   150

    Princess. Therefore I do it; and I make no doubt
The rest will ne'er come in if he be out.
There 's no such sport as sport by sport o'erthrown,
To make theirs ours, and ours none but our own;
So shall we stay, mocking intended game,
And they, well mock'd, depart away with shame.

                       [*Trumpets sound within.*

    Boyet. The trumpet sounds: be mask'd; the mask-
        ers come.   [*The Ladies mask.*

Enter Blackamoors with music; MOTH; *the* KING, BI-
RON, LONGAVILLE, *and* DUMAIN, *in Russian habits,
and masked*

Moth.   All hail, the richest beauties on the earth!

Boyet.   Beauties no richer than rich taffeta.

Moth.   A holy parcel of the fairest dames   160
                    [*The Ladies turn their backs to him.*
That ever turn'd their — backs — to mortal views!

Biron.   [*Aside to Moth*] Their eyes, villain, their
          eyes.

Moth.   That ever turn'd their eyes to mortal views! —
Out —

Boyet.   True; out indeed.

Moth.   Out of your favours, heavenly spirits, vouchsafe
Not to behold —

Biron.   [*Aside to Moth*] Once to behold, rogue.

Moth.   Once to behold with your sun-beamed eyes,
—— with your sun-beamed eyes —   170

Boyet.   They will not answer to that epithet;
You were best call it daughter-beamed eyes.

Moth.   They do not mark me, and that brings me out.

Biron.   Is this your perfectness? be gone, you
          rogue!   [*Exit Moth.*

Rosaline.   What would these strangers? know their
          minds, Boyet.
If they do speak our language, 't is our will
That some plain man recount their purposes.
Know what they would.

Boyet. What would you with the princess?

Biron. Nothing but peace and gentle visitation. 180

Rosaline. What would they, say they.?

Boyet. Nothing but peace and gentle visitation.

Rosaline. Why, that they have; and bid them **so**
be gone.

Boyet. She says, you have it, and you may be gone.

King. Say to her, we have measur'd many miles
To tread a measure with her on this grass.

Boyet. They say that they have measur'd many a
mile
To tread a measure with you on this grass.

Rosaline. It is not so. Ask them how many inches
Is in one mile; if they have measur'd many, 190
The measure then of one is easily told.

Boyet. If to come hither you have measur'd miles,
And many miles, the princess bids you tell
How many inches doth fill up one mile.

Biron. Tell her, we measure them by weary steps.

Boyet. She hears herself.

Rosaline. How many weary steps,
Of many weary miles you have o'ergone,
Are number'd in the travel of one mile?

Biron. We number nothing that we spend for you;
Our duty is so rich, so infinite, 200
That we may do it still without accompt.
Vouchsafe to show the sunshine of your face,
That we, like savages, may worship it.

Rosaline. My face is but a moon, and clouded too.

King. Blessed are clouds, to do as such clouds do!
Vouchsafe, bright moon, — and these thy stars, — to
      shine,
Those clouds remov'd, upon our watery eyne.

Rosaline. O vain petitioner! beg a greater matter;
Thou now request'st but moonshine in the water.

King. Then, in our measure vouchsafe but one
      change.   210
Thou bidst me beg; this begging is not strange.

Rosaline. Play, music, then! — Nay, you must do it
      soon.   [*Music plays.*
Not yet, — no dance! — Thus change I like the moon.

King. Will you not dance? How come you thus
      estrang'd?

Rosaline. You took the moon at full, but now she 's
      chang'd.

King. Yet still she is the moon, and I the man.
The music plays; vouchsafe some motion to it.

Rosaline. Our ears vouchsafe it.

King.   But your legs should do it.

Rosaline. Since you are strangers and come here by
      chance,   219
We 'll not be nice; take hands. — We will not dance.

King. Why take we hands, then?

Rosaline.   Only to part friends.
Curtsy, sweet hearts; and so the measure ends.

King. More measure of this measure; be not
      nice.

Rosaline. We can afford no more at such a price.

King. Prize you yourselves; what buys your company?

Rosaline. Your absence only.

King.   That can never be.

Rosaline. Then cannot we be bought; and so, adieu,
Twice to your visor and half once to you.

King. If you deny to dance, let's hold more chat.

Rosaline. In private, then.

King.   I am best pleas'd with that.

                                   [*They converse apart.*

Biron. White-handed mistress, one sweet word with
thee.   231

Princess. Honey, and milk, and sugar; there is
three.

Biron. Nay then, two treys, and if you grow so nice,
Metheglin, wort, and malmsey.   Well run, dice!
There's half-a-dozen sweets.

Princess.   Seventh sweet, adieu.
Since you can cog, I'll play no more with you.

Biron. One word in secret.

Princess.   Let it not be sweet.

Biron. Thou griev'st my gall.

Princess.   Gall! bitter.

Biron.   Therefore meet.

                                   [*They converse apart.*

Dumain. Will you vouchsafe with me to change a
word?

Maria. Name it.

Dumain.   Fair lady, —

Maria.   Say you so? Fair lord,—
Take that for your fair lady.

Dumain.   Please it you,   241
As much in private, and I 'll bid adieu.

                              [*They converse apart.*

  Katherine. What, was your vizard made without a
        tongue?

  Longaville. I know the reason, lady, why you ask.

  Katherine. O, for your reason! quickly, sir; I long.

  Longaville. You have a double tongue within your
        mask,
And would afford my speechless vizard half.

  Katherine. Veal, quoth the Dutchman.— Is not veal
        a calf?

  Longaville. A calf, fair lady!

  Katherine.   No, a fair lord calf.

  Longaville. Let 's part the word.

  Katherine.   No, I 'll not be your half.
Take all, and wean it; it may prove an ox.   251

  Longaville. Look, how you butt yourself in these
        sharp mocks!
Will you give horns, chaste lady? do not so.

  Katherine. Then die, a calf, before your horns do
        grow.

  Longaville. One word in private with you, ere I die.

  Katherine. Bleat softly then; the butcher hears you
        cry.   [*They converse apart.*

  Boyet. The tongues of mocking wenches are as keen
As is the razor's edge invisible,

Cutting a smaller hair than may be seen;
  Above the sense of sense, so sensible   260
Seemeth their conference; their conceits have wings
Fleeter than arrows, bullets, wind, thought, swifter
      things.

  Rosaline. Not one word more, my maids; break off,
    break off.

  Biron. By heaven, all dry-beaten with pure scoff!

  King. Farewell, mad wenches; you have simple
    wits.

  Princess. Twenty adieus, my frozen Muscovits. —
           [*Exeunt King, Lords, and Blackamoors.*
Are these the breed of wits so wonder'd at?

  Boyet. Tapers they are, with your sweet breaths
    puff'd out.

  Rosaline. Well-liking wits they have; gross, gross,
    fat, fat.

  Princess. O poverty in wit, kingly-poor flout!   270
Will they not, think you, hang themselves to-night?
Or ever, but in vizards, show their faces?
This pert Biron was out of countenance quite.

  Rosaline. O, they were all in lamentable cases!
The king was weeping-ripe for a good word.

  Princess. Biron did swear himself out of all suit.

  Maria. Dumain was at my service, and his sword.
No point, quoth I; my servant straight was mute.

  Katherine. Lord Longaville said I came o'er his heart;
And trow you what he call'd me?

  Princess.   Qualm, perhaps.

Katherine.   Yes, in good faith.

Princess.   Go, sickness as thou art!

Rosaline.   Well, better wits have worn plain statute-
        caps.   282

But will you hear? the king is my love sworn.

Princess.   And quick Biron hath plighted faith to me.

Katherine.   And Longaville was for my service born.

Maria.   Dumain is mine, as sure as bark on tree.

Boyet.   Madam—and pretty mistresses—give ear.

Immediately they will again be here

In their own shapes; for it can never be

They will digest this harsh indignity.   290

Princess.   Will they return?

Boyet.   They will, they will, God knows,

And leap for joy, though they are lame with blows.

Therefore change favours; and, when they repair,

Blow like sweet roses in this summer air.

Princess.   How blow? how blow? speak to be under-
        stood.

Boyet.   Fair ladies mask'd are roses in their bud;

Dismask'd, their damask sweet commixture shown,

Are angels vailing clouds, or roses blown.

Princess.   Avaunt, perplexity!   What shall we do,

If they return in their own shapes to woo?   301

Rosaline.   Good madam, if by me you'll be advis'd,

Let's mock them still, as well known as disguis'd.

Let us complain to them what fools were here,

Disguis'd like Muscovites, in shapeless gear,

And wonder what they were, and to what end

Their shallow shows, and prologue vilely penn'd,
And their rough carriage so ridiculous,
Should be presented at our tent to us.   309

   Boyet. Ladies, withdraw; the gallants are at hand.

   Princess. Whip to our tents, as roes run over land.

   [*Exeunt Princess, Rosaline, Katherine, and Maria.*

Re-enter the KING, BIRON, LONGAVILLE, *and* DUMAIN,
    in their proper habits

   King. Fair sir, God save you! Where's the princess ?

   Boyet. Gone to her tent. Please it your majesty
Command me any service to her thither ?

   King. That she vouchsafe me audience for one word.

   Boyet. I will; and so will she, I know, my lord. [*Exit.*

   Biron. This fellow pecks up wit as pigeons pease,
And utters it again when God doth please.
He is wit's pedler, and retails his wares
At wakes and wassails, meetings, markets, fairs;   320
And we that sell by gross, the Lord doth know,
Have not the grace to grace it with such show.
This gallant pins the wenches on his sleeve ;
Had he been Adam, he had tempted Eve.
He can carve too, and lisp ; why, this is he
That kiss'd his hand away in courtesy ;
This is the ape of form, monsieur the nice,
That, when he plays at tables, chides the dice
In honourable terms ; nay, he can sing
A mean most meanly ; and in ushering   330

Mend him who can? the ladies call him sweet;
The stairs, as he treads on them, kiss his feet.
This is the flower that smiles on every one,
To show his teeth as white as whale's bone;
And consciences that will not die in debt
Pay him the due of honey-tongu'd Boyet.

    King. A blister on his sweet tongue, with my heart,
That put Armado's page out of his part!

    Biron. See where it comes! — Behaviour, what wert
        thou
Till this man show'd thee? and what art thou now? 340

Re-enter the Princess, *ushered by* Boyet; Rosaline,
    Maria, *and* Katherine

    King. All hail, sweet madame, and fair time of day!
    Princess. Fair in all hail is foul, as I conceive.
    King. Construe my speeches better, if you may.
    Princess. Then wish me better; I will give you
        leave.
    King. We came to visit you, and purpose now
To lead you to our court; vouchsafe it then.
    Princess. This field shall hold me, and so hold your
        vow;
Nor God, nor I, delights in perjur'd men.
    King. Rebuke me not for that which you provoke;
The virtue of your eye must break my oath.   350
    Princess. You nickname virtue; vice you should have
        spoke,
For virtue's office never breaks men's troth.

Now by my maiden honour, yet as pure
  As the unsullied lily, I protest,
A world of torments though I should endure,
  I would not yield to be your house's guest,
So much I hate a breaking cause to be
Of heavenly oaths, vow'd with integrity.

  King. O, you have liv'd in desolation here,   360
    Unseen, unvisited, much to our shame.
  Princess. Not so, my lord; it is not so, I swear;
    We have had pastimes here and pleasant game.
A mess of Russians left us but of late.
  King. How, madam! Russians!
  Princess.   Ay, in truth, my lord;
Trim gallants, full of courtship and of state.
  Rosaline. Madam, speak true. — It is not so, my lord;
My lady, to the manner of the days,
In courtesy gives undeserving praise.
We four indeed confronted were with four
In Russian habit; here they stay'd an hour   370
And talk'd apace, and in that hour, my lord,
They did not bless us with one happy word.
I dare not call them fools; but this I think,
When they are thirsty, fools would fain have drink.
  Biron. This jest is dry to me. — Fair gentle sweet,
Your wit makes wise things foolish. When we greet,
With eyes best seeing, heaven's fiery eye,
By light we lose light; your capacity
Is of that nature that to your huge store
Wise things seem foolish and rich things but poor.   380

Rosaline. This proves you wise and rich, for in my
    eye, —

Biron. I am a fool, and full of poverty.

Rosaline. But that you take what doth to you belong,
It were a fault to snatch words from my tongue.

Biron. O, I am yours, and all that I possess!

Rosaline. All the fool mine?

Biron.   I cannot give you less.

Rosaline. Which of the vizards was it that you wore?

Biron. Where? when? what vizard? why demand
    you this?

Rosaline. There, then, that vizard; that superfluous
    case
That hid the worse and show'd the better face.   390

King. [*Aside to Dumain*] We are descried; they'll
    mock us now downright.

Dumain. [*Aside to King*] Let us confess and turn it
    to a jest.

Princess. Amaz'd, my lord? why looks your highness
    sad?

Rosaline. Help, hold his brows! he'll swoon! —
    Why look you pale? —
Sea-sick, I think, coming from Muscovy.

Biron. Thus pour the stars down plagues for perjury.
Can any face of brass hold longer out? —
Here stand I, lady, dart thy skill at me;
    Bruise me with scorn, confound me with a flout;
Thrust thy sharp wit quite through my ignorance;   400
    Cut me to pieces with thy keen conceit;

And I will wish thee never more to dance,
  Nor never more in Russian habit wait.
O, never will I trust to speeches penn'd,
  Nor to the motion of a schoolboy's tongue,
Nor never come in vizard to my friend,
  Nor woo in rhyme, like a blind harper's song!
Taffeta phrases, silken terms precise,
  Three-pil'd hyperboles, spruce affectation,
Figures pedantical — these summer-flies   410
  Have blown me full of maggot ostentation.
I do forswear them, and I here protest,
  By this white glove, — how white the hand, God
      knows! —
Henceforth my wooing mind shall be express'd
  In russet yeas and honest kersey noes;
And to begin, wench, — so God help me, la! —
My love to thee is sound, sans crack or flaw.
  Rosaline. Sans sans, I pray you.
  Biron.   Yet I have a trick
Of the old rage; bear with me, I am sick;
I'll leave it by degrees. Soft, let us see: 420
Write, 'Lord have mercy on us' on those three;
They are infected, in their hearts it lies;
They have the plague, and caught it of your eyes;
These lords are visited; you are not free,
For the Lord's tokens on you do I see.
  Princess. No, they are free that gave these tokens to
      us.
  Biron. Our states are forfeit; seek not to undo us.

Rosaline. It is not so ; for how can this be true,
That you stand forfeit, being those that sue ?

Biron. Peace ! for I will not have to do with you.

Rosaline. Nor shall not, if I do as I intend.   431

Biron. Speak for yourselves ; my wit is at an end.

King. Teach us, sweet madam, for our rude transgression
Some fair excuse.

Princess.   The fairest is confession.
Were not you here but even now disguis'd ?

King. Madam, I was.

Princess.   And were you well advis'd ?

King. I was, fair madam.

Princess.   When you then were here,
What did you whisper in your lady's ear ?

King. That more than all the world I did respect
her.

Princess. When she shall challenge this, you will re-
ject her.   440

King. Upon mine honour, no.

Princess.   Peace, peace ! forbear ;
Your oath once broke, you force not to forswear.

King. Despise me when I break this oath of mine.

Princess. I will ; and therefore keep it. — Rosaline,
What did the Russian whisper in your ear ?

Rosaline. Madam, he swore that he did hold me dear
As precious eyesight, and did value me
Above this world ; adding thereto moreover
That he would wed me or else die my lover.

Princess. God give thee joy of him ! the noble lord
Most honourably doth uphold his word.   451

King. What mean you, madam ? by my life, my
            troth,
I never swore this lady such an oath.

Rosaline. By heaven, you did, and to confirm it plain,
You gave me this ; but take it, sir, again.

King. My faith and this the princess I did give ;
I knew her by this jewel on her sleeve.

Princess. Pardon me, sir, this jewel did she wear ;
And Lord Biron, I thank him, is my dear. —
What, will you have me, or your pearl again ?   460

Biron. Neither of either ; I remit both twain. —
I see the trick on 't ; here was a consent,
Knowing aforehand of our merriment,
To dash it like a Christmas comedy.
Some carry-tale, some please-man, some slight zany,
Some mumble-news, some trencher-knight, some Dick,
That smiles his cheek in years and knows the trick
To make my lady laugh when she 's dispos'd,
Told our intents before ; which once disclos'd,
The ladies did change favours, and then we,   470
Following the signs, woo'd but the sign of she.
Now, to our perjury to add more terror,
We are again forsworn, — in will, and error.
Much upon this it is. — And might not you   [*To Boyet.*
Forestall our sport, to make us thus untrue ?
Do not you know my lady's foot by the squire,
    And laugh upon the apple of her eye ?

And stand between her back, sir, and the fire,
   Holding a trencher, jesting merrily?
You put our page out; go, you are allow'd;   480
Die when you will, a smock shall be your shroud.
You leer upon me, do you? there 's an eye
Wounds like a leaden sword.
   Boyet.   Full merrily
Hath this brave manage, this career, been run.
   Biron. Lo, he is tilting straight! Peace! I have
      done. —

Enter COSTARD

Welcome, pure wit! thou partest a fair fray.
   Costard. O Lord, sir, they would know
Whether the three Worthies shall come in or no.
   Biron. What, are there but three?
   Costard.   No, sir; but it is vara fine,
For every one pursents three.
   Biron.   And three times thrice is nine.
   Costard. Not so, sir; under correction, sir; I hope it
      is not so.   491
You cannot beg us, sir, I can assure you, sir, we know
      what we know;
I hope, sir, three times thrice, sir, —
   Biron. Is not nine.
   Costard. Under correction, sir, we know where-
until it doth amount.
   Biron. By Jove, I always took three threes for
      nine.

Costard. O Lord, sir, it were pity you should get your living by reckoning, sir.

Biron. How much is it?   500

Costard. O Lord, sir, the parties themselves, the actors, sir, will show whereuntil it doth amount; for mine own part, I am, as they say, but to pursent one man, — e'en one poor man — Pompion the **Great**, sir.

Biron. Art thou one of the Worthies?

Costard. It pleased them to think me worthy of Pompion the Great; for mine own part, I know not the degree of the Worthy, but I am to stand for him.

Biron. Go, bid them prepare.   510

Costard. We will turn it finely off, sir; we will take
    some care.   [*Exit.*

King. Biron, they will shame us; let them not ap-
    proach.

Biron. We are shame-proof, my lord; and 't is some
    policy
To have one show worse than the king's and his com
    pany.

King. I say they shall not come.

Princess. Nay, my good lord, let me o'errule you
    now;
That sport best pleases that dost least know how.
Where zeal strives to content, and the contents
Dies in the zeal of that which it presents,
Their form confounded makes most form in mirth,   520
When great things labouring perish in their birth.

Biron. A right description of our sport, my lord.

Enter ARMADO

Armado. Anointed, I implore so much expense of thy royal sweet breath as will utter a brace of words.
    [*Converses apart with the King and delivers him a paper.*

Princess. Doth this man serve God?

Biron. Why ask you?

Princess. He speaks not like a man of God's making.   528

Armado. That is all one, my fair, sweet, honey monarch, for, I protest, the schoolmaster is exceeding fantastical, too-too vain, too-too vain; but we will put it, as they say, to fortuna de la guerra. I wish you the peace of mind, most royal couplement! [*Exit.*

King. Here is like to be a good presence of Worthies. He presents Hector of Troy; the swain, Pompey the Great; the parish curate, Alexander; Armado's page, Hercules; the pedant, Judas Maccabæus:
And if these four Worthies in their first show thrive,
These four will change habits, and present the other five.

Biron. There is five in the first show.   541

King. You are deceived; 't is not so.

Biron. The pedant, the braggart, the hedge-priest, the fool, and the boy. —
Abate throw at novum, and the whole world again
Cannot prick out five such, take each one in his vein.

King. The ship is under sail, and here she comes
  amain.

Enter COSTARD, *for Pompey*

Costard. I Pompey am,—
Boyet.   You lie, you are not he.
Costard. I Pompey am,—
Boyet.   With libbard's head on knee.
Biron. Well said, old mocker; I must needs be
  friends with thee.
Costard. I Pompey am, Pompey surnam'd the Big,—   551
Dumain. The Great.
Costard. It is Great, sir:—

                    Pompey surnam'd the Great,
That oft in field, with targe and shield, did make my foe to
  sweat;
And travelling along this coast, I here am come by chance,
And lay my arms before the legs of this sweet lass of France.—
If your ladyship would say, 'Thanks, Pompey,' I had
  done.
Princess. Great thanks, great Pompey.
Costard. 'T is not so much worth; but I hope I
was perfect. I made a little fault in 'Great.'
Biron. My hat to a halfpenny, Pompey proves
the best Worthy.   562

Enter SIR NATHANIEL, *for Alexander*

Nathaniel. When in the world I liv'd, I was the world's
  commander;
      LOVE'S LABOUR — 9

By east, west, north, and south, I spread my conquering might ;
My scutcheon plain declares that I am Alisander, —

    Boyet. Your nose says, no, you are not; for it
       stands too right.

    Biron. Your nose smells no in this, most tender-
       smelling knight.

    Princess. The conqueror is dismay'd. — Proceed,
       good Alexander.

    Nathaniel. When in the world I liv'd, I was the world's com-
       mander, —

    Boyet. Most true, 't is right ; you were so, Alisander.

    Biron. Pompey the Great, —   571

    Costard. Your servant, and Costard.

    Biron. Take away the conqueror, take away Ali-
sander.

    Costard. [*To Sir Nathaniel*] O, sir, you have
overthrown Alisander the conqueror ! You will be
scraped out of the painted cloth for this ; your lion,
that holds his poll-axe sitting on a close-stool, will be
given to Ajax ; he will be the ninth Worthy. A conqueror, and afeard to speak ! run away for shame, 580
Alisander. — [*Nathaniel retires.*] There, an 't shall
please you ; a foolish mild man, an honest man, look
you, and soon dashed. He is a marvellous good
neighbour, faith, and a very good bowler ; but, for
Alisander, — alas, you see how 't is, — a little o'erparted. — But there are Worthies a-coming will
speak their mind in some other sort.

    Princess. Stand aside, good Pompey.

Enter HOLOFERNES, *for Judas; and* MOTH, *for Hercules*

Holofernes. Great Hercules is presented by this imp,
  Whose club kill'd Cerberus, that three-headed canus ;   590
  And when he was a babe, a child, a shrimp,
  Thus did he strangle serpents in his manus.
  Quoniam he seemeth in minority,
  Ergo I come with this apology. —

Keep some state in thy exit, and vanish. — [*Moth retires.*
  Judas I am, —

Dumain. A Judas !

Holofernes. Not Iscariot, sir. —
  Judas I am, ycliped Maccabæus.

Dumain. Judas Maccabæus clipt is plain Judas.   600

Biron. A kissing traitor. — How art thou prov'd Judas?

Holofernes. Judas I am, —

Dumain. The more shame for you, Judas.

Holofernes. What mean you, sir ?

Boyet. To make Judas hang himself.

Holofernes. Begin, sir ; you are my elder.

Biron. Well follow'd ; Judas was hang'd on an elder.

Holofernes. I will not be put out of countenance.

Biron. Because thou hast no face.

Holofernes. What is this ?   610

Boyet. A cittern-head.

Dumain. The head of a bodkin.

Biron. A death's face in a ring.

Longaville. The face of an old Roman coin, scarce seen.

Boyet. The pommel of Cæsar's falchion.

Dumain. The carved-bone face on a flask.

Biron. Saint George's half-cheek in a brooch.

Dumain. Ay, and in a brooch of lead.

Biron. Ay, and worn in the cap of a tooth-drawer. —
And now forward; for we have put thee in counte-
        nance.   620

Holofernes. You have put me out of countenance.

Biron. False; we have given thee faces.

Holofernes. But you have out-faced them all.

Biron. An thou wert a lion, we would do so.

Boyet. Therefore, as he is an ass, let him go. —
And so adieu, sweet Jude! nay, why dost thou stay?

Dumain. For the latter end of his name,

Biron. For the ass to the Jude? give it him. —
        Jud-as, away!

Holofernes. This is not generous, not gentle, not
        humble.

Boyet. A light for Monsieur Judas! it grows dark,
        he may stumble.   [*Holofernes retires.*

Princess. Alas, poor Maccabæus, how hath he been
        baited!   631

Enter ARMADO, *for Hector*

Biron. Hide thy head, Achilles; here comes
Hector in arms.

Dumain. Though my mocks come home by me,
I will now be merry.

King. Hector was but a Trojan in respect of this.

Boyet. But is this Hector?

King. I think Hector was not so clean-timbered.

Longaville. His leg is too big for Hector's.

Dumain. More calf, certain.   640

Boyet. No; he is best indued in the small.

Biron. This cannot be Hector.

Dumain. He's a god or a painter; for he makes faces.

Armado. The armipotent Mars, of lances the almighty,
　Gave Hector a gift, —

Dumain. A gilt nutmeg.

Biron. A lemon.

Longaville. Stuck with cloves.

Dumain. No, cloven.   650

Armado. Peace! —

The armipotent Mars, of lances the almighty,
　Gave Hector a gift, the heir of Ilion;
A man so breath'd that certain he would fight ye
　From morn till night, out of his pavilion.

I am that flower, —

Dumain.　　　　　That mint.

Longaville.　　　　　　　　　That columbine.

Armado. Sweet Lord Longaville, rein thy tongue.

Longaville. I must rather give it the rein, for it runs against Hector.

Dumain. Ay, and Hector's a greyhound.   660

Armado. The sweet war-man is dead and rotten. Sweet chucks, beat not the bones of the buried; when he breathed, he was a man. But I will for-

ward with my device. — [*To the Princess*] Sweet
royalty, bestow on me the sense of hearing.

Princess. Speak, brave Hector; we are much delighted.

Armado. I do adore thy sweet grace's slipper.

Boyet. [*Aside to Dumain*] Loves her by the foot.

Dumain. [*Aside to Boyet*] He may not by the yard.

Armado. This Hector far surmounted Hannibal, —   671

Costard. The party is gone, fellow Hector, she is
gone; she is two months on her way.

Armado. What meanest thou?

Costard. Faith, unless you play the honest Trojan, the poor wench is cast away; she 's quick.

Armado. Dost thou infamonize me among poten-
tates? thou shalt die.

Costard. Then shall Hector be whipped for Jaquenetta that is quick by him, and hanged for Pompey
that is dead by him.   68»

Dumain. Most rare Pompey!

Boyet. Renowned Pompey!

Biron. Greater than great, — great, great, great
Pompey! Pompey the Huge!

Dumain. Hector trembles.

Biron. Pompey is moved. — More Ates! stir
them on! stir them on!

Dumain. Hector will challenge him.

Biron. Ay, if he have no more man's blood in 's
belly than will sup a flea.   69»

Armado. By the north pole, I do challenge thee.

Costard. I will not fight with a pole, like a northern man; I 'll slash, I 'll do it by the sword. I pray you, let me borrow my arms again.

Dumain. Room for the incensed Worthies.

Costard. I 'll do it in my shirt.

Dumain. Most resolute Pompey!

Moth. Master, let me take you a buttonhole lower. Do you see Pompey is uncasing for the combat? What mean you? You will lose your reputation.

Armado. Gentlemen and soldiers, pardon me; I will not combat in my shirt.   703

Dumain. You may not deny it; Pompey hath made the challenge.

Armado. Sweet bloods, I both may and will.

Biron. What reason have you for 't?

Armado. The naked truth of it is, I have no shirt; I go woolward for penance.

Boyet. True, and it was enjoined him in Rome for want of linen; since when, I 'll be sworn, he wore none but a dishclout of Jaquenetta's, and that he wears next his heart for a favour.   713

Enter MERCADE

Mercade. God save you, madam!

Princess. Welcome, Mercade,
But that thou interrupt'st our merriment.

Mercade. I am sorry, madam, for the news I bring
Is heavy in my tongue. The king your father —

Princess. Dead, for my life!

Mercade.   Even so; my tale is told.

Biron. Worthies, away! the scene begins to cloud. 720

Armado. For mine own part, I breathe free breath.
I have seen the day of wrong through the little hole of
discretion, and I will right myself like a soldier.

                              [*Exeunt Worthies.*

King. How fares your majesty?

Princess. Boyet, prepare; I will away to-night.

King. Madam, not so; I do beseech you, stay.

Princess. Prepare, I say. — I thank you gracious
        lords,
For all your fair endeavours, and entreat,
Out of a new-sad soul, that you vouchsafe
In your rich wisdom to excuse or hide   730
The liberal opposition of our spirits;
If over-boldly we have borne ourselves
In the converse of breath, your gentleness
Was guilty of it. — Farewell, worthy lord!
A heavy heart bears not a humble tongue.
Excuse me so, coming too short of thanks
For my great suit so easily obtain'd.

  King. The extreme parts of time extremely forms
All causes to the purpose of his speed,
And often at his very loose decides   740
That which long process could not arbitrate;
And though the mourning brow of progeny
Forbid the smiling courtesy of love
The holy suit which fain it would convince,
Yet, since love's argument was first on foot,

Let not the cloud of sorrow justle it
From what it purpos'd, since to wail friends lost
Is not by much so wholesome-profitable
As to rejoice at friends but newly found.

   Princess. I understand you not; my griefs are
    dull.   750

   Biron. Honest plain words best pierce the ear of
    grief;

And by these badges understand the king.
For your fair sakes have we neglected time,
Play'd foul play with our oaths. Your beauty, ladies,
Hath much deform'd us, fashioning our humours
Even to the opposed end of our intents;
And what in us hath seem'd ridiculous, —
As love is full of unbefitting strains,
All wanton as a child, skipping and vain,
Form'd by the eye, and therefore, like the eye,   760
Full of strange shapes, of habits, and of forms,
Varying in subjects as the eye doth roll
To every varied object in his glance, —
Which parti-coated presence of loose love
Put on by us, if, in your heavenly eyes,
Have misbecom'd our oaths and gravities,
Those heavenly eyes that look into these faults
Suggested us to make. Therefore, ladies,
Our love being yours, the error that love makes
Is likewise yours. We to ourselves prove false,   770
By being once false for ever to be true
To those that make us both, — fair ladies, you;

And even that falsehood, in itself a sin,
Thus purifies itself and turns to grace.

 Princess. We have receiv'd your letters full of love,
Your favours, the ambassadors of love,
And in our maiden council rated them
At courtship, pleasant jest, and courtesy,
As bombast and as lining to the time ;
But more devout than this in our respects   780
Have we not been, and therefore met your loves
In their own fashion, like a merriment.

 Dumain. Our letters, madam, show'd much more
   than jest.

 Longaville. So did our looks.

 Rosaline.   We did not quote them so.

 King. Now, at the latest minute of the hour,
Grant us your loves.

 Princess.   A time, methinks, too short
To make a world-without-end bargain in.
No, no, my lord, your grace is perjur'd much,
Full of dear guiltiness ; and therefore this :
If for my love — as there is no such cause —   790
You will do aught, this shall you do for me :
Your oath I will not trust, but go with speed
To some forlorn and naked hermitage,
Remote from all the pleasures of the world ;
There stay until the twelve celestial signs
Have brought about the annual reckoning.
If this austere insociable life
Change not your offer made in heat of blood,

If frosts and fasts, hard lodging and thin weeds
Nip not the gaudy blossoms of your love   800
But that it bear this trial and last love,
Then, at the expiration of the year,
Come challenge me, challenge me by these deserts,
And, by this virgin palm now kissing thine,
I will be thine, and till that instant shut
My woeful self up in a mourning house,
Raining the tears of lamentation
For the remembrance of my father's death.
If this thou do deny, let our hands part,
Neither intitled in the other's heart.   810

    King. If this, or more than this, I would deny,
    To flatter up these powers of mine with rest,
The sudden hand of death close up mine eye !
    Hence ever then my heart is in thy breast.

    [*Biron.* And what to me, my love ? and what to me ?
    Rosaline. You must be purged too, your sins are
      rank,
You are attaint with faults and perjury ;
Therefore if you my favour mean to get,
A twelvemonth shall you spend, and never rest,
But seek the weary beds of people sick.]   820

    Dumain. But what to me, my love? but what to me ?
A wife ?
    Katherine. A beard, fair health, and honesty ;
With three-fold love I wish you all these three.
    Dumain. O, shall I say, I thank you, gentle wife?
    Katherine. Not so, my lord ; a twelvemonth and a day

I 'll mark no words that smooth-fac'd wooers say.

Come when the king doth to my lady come;

Then, if I have much love, I 'll give you some.

    Dumain. I 'll serve thee true and faithfully till then.

    Katherine. Yet swear not, lest ye be forsworn again.

    Longaville. What says Maria?

    Maria.   At the twelvemonth's end

I 'll change my black gown for a faithful friend.   832

    Longaville. I 'll stay with patience; but the time is

        long.

    Maria. The liker you; few taller are so young.

    Biron. Studies my lady? mistress, look on me;

Behold the window of my heart, mine eye,

What humble suit attends thy answer there.

Impose some service on me for thy love.

    Rosaline. Oft have I heard of you, my Lord Biron,

Before I saw you; and the world's large tongue   840

Proclaims you for a man replete with mocks,

Full of comparisons and wounding flouts,

Which you on all estates will execute

That lie within the mercy of your wit.

To weed this wormwood from your fruitful brain,

And therewithal to win me, if you please, —

Without the which I am not to be won, —

You shall this twelvemonth term from day to day

Visit the speechless sick, and still converse

With groaning wretches; and your task shall be,   850

With all the fierce endeavour of your wit

To enforce the pained impotent to smile.

Biron. To move wild laughter in the throat of
    death?
It cannot be, it is impossible;
Mirth cannot move a soul in agony.

    Rosaline. Why, that's the way to choke a gibing
       spirit,
Whose influence is begot of that loose grace
Which shallow laughing hearers give to fools.
A jest's prosperity lies in the ear
Of him that hears it, never in the tongue   860
Of him that makes it. Then, if sickly ears,
Deaf'd with the clamours of their own dear groans,
Will hear your idle scorns, continue them,
And I will have you and that fault withal;
But if they will not, throw away that spirit,
And I shall find you empty of that fault,
Right joyful of your reformation.

    Biron. A twelvemonth! well; befall what will be-
    fall,
I 'll jest a twelvemonth in an hospital.

    Princess. [*To the King*] Ay, sweet my lord; and so I
    take my leave.   870

    King. No, madam; we will bring you on your
    way.

    Biron. Our wooing doth not end like an old play,
Jack hath not Jill; these ladies' courtesy
Might well have made our sport a comedy.

    King. Come, sir, it wants a twelvemonth and a day,
And then 't will end.

Biron.   That's too long for a play.

Re-enter ARMADO

Armado. Sweet majesty, vouchsafe me, —
Princess. Was not that Hector?
Dumain. The worthy knight of Troy.   879
Armado. I will kiss thy royal finger, and take leave. I am a votary; I have vowed to Jaquenetta to hold the plough for her sweet love three years. But, most esteemed greatness, will you hear the dialogue that the two learned men have compiled in praise of the owl and the cuckoo? it should have followed in the end of our show.
King. Call them forth quickly; we will do so.
Armado. Holla! approach. —

Re-enter HOLOFERNES, NATHANIEL, MOTH, COSTARD, *and others*

This side is Hiems, Winter, this Ver, the Spring; the one maintained by the owl, the other by the cuckoo. — Ver, begin.   891

Song

Spring.   *When daisies pied and violets blue,*
              And lady-smocks all silver-white,
              And cuckoo-buds of yellow hue
                 Do paint the meadows with delight,
              The cuckoo then, on every tree,
              Mocks married men, for thus sings he,
                 Cuckoo;

Cuckoo, cuckoo, — O word of fear,
　Unpleasing to a married ear!　　　900

When shepherds pipe on oaten straws,
　　And merry larks are ploughmen's clocks,
When turtles tread, and rooks and daws,
　　And maidens bleach their summer smocks,
The cuckoo then, on every tree,
Mocks married men, for thus sings he,
　　　　　　Cuckoo;
Cuckoo, cuckoo, — O word of fear,
　Unpleasing to a married ear!　　　909

Winter.　*When icicles hang by the wall,*
　　And Dick the shepherd blows his nail,
And Tom bears logs into the hall,
　　And milk comes frozen home in pail,
When blood is nipp'd and ways be foul,
Then nightly sings the staring owl,
　　　　　　Tu-whoo;
Tu-whit, tu-whoo, a merry note,
While greasy Joan doth keel the pot.　　918

When all aloud the wind doth blow,
　　And coughing drowns the parson's saw,
And birds sit brooding in the snow,
　　And Marian's nose looks red and raw,
When roasted crabs hiss in the bowl,
Then nightly sings the staring owl,
　　　　　　Tu-whoo;

Tu-whit, tu-whoo, a merry note,
  While greasy Joan doth keel the pot.   927

Armado. The words of Mercury are harsh after the songs of Apollo. — You that way, — we this way.
  [*Exeunt.*

NOTES

RUSSIAN COSTUMES OF THE PERIOD

NOTES

INTRODUCTION

THE METRE OF THE PLAY. — It should be understood at the outset that *metre*, or the mechanism of verse, is something altogether distinct from the *music* of verse. The one is matter of rule, the other of taste and feeling. Music is not an absolute necessity of verse; the metrical form is a necessity, being that which constitutes the verse.

The plays of Shakespeare (with the exception of rhymed passages, and of occasional songs and interludes) are all in unrhymed or *blank* verse; and the normal form of this blank verse is illustrated by i. 1. 19 of the present play : "Your oaths are pass'd; and now subscribe your names."

This line, it will be seen, consists of ten syllables, with the even syllables (2d, 4th, 6th, 8th, and 10th) accented, the odd syllables

(1st, 3d, etc.) being unaccented.   Theoretically, it is made up of five *feet* of two syllables each, with the accent on the second sylla-ble.   Such a foot is called an *iambus* (plural, *iambuses*, or the Latin *iambi*), and the form of verse is called *iambic.*

This fundamental law of Shakespeare's verse is subject to certain modifications, the most important of which are as follows : —

1. After the tenth syllable an unaccented syllable (or even two such syllables) may be added, forming what is sometimes called a *female* line; as in i. 1. 17 : "My fellow scholars, and to keep those statutes."   The rhythm is complete with the first syllable of *statutes*, the second being an extra eleventh syllable.   See also lines 94, 95, 96, 97, etc.

2. The accent in any part of the verse may be shifted from an even to an odd syllable; as in i. 1. 48 : "Not to see ladies, study, fast, not sleep !" and 55 : "What is the end of study ? let me know."   In both lines the accent is shifted from the second to the first syllable.   This change occurs very rarely in the tenth syllable, and seldom in the fourth ; and it is not allowable in two succes-sive accented syllables.

3. An extra unaccented syllable may occur in any part of the line ; as in i. 1. 5 and 109.   In 5 the first syllable of *endeavour* is superfluous ; and in 109 that of *unlock*.   In line 140 (a female line) the first syllable of *admired* (or the word *the*) is superfluous.

4. Any unaccented syllable, occurring in an even place immedi-ately before or after an even syllable which is properly accented, is reckoned as accented for the purposes of the verse ; as, for instance, in lines 2 and 4.   In 2 the last syllable of *register'd*, and in 4 that of *cormorant*, are metrically equivalent to accented syllables ; and so with the last syllable of *eternity* in 7 and of *conquerors* in 8.

5. In many instances in Shakespeare words must be *lengthened* in order to fill out the rhythm : —

(*a*) In a large class of words in which *e* or *i* is followed by an-other vowel, the *e* or *i* is made a separate syllable ; as *ocean*, *opin-ion*, *soldier*, *patience*, *partial*, *marriage*, etc.   For instance, line 9 of the first scene ("That was against your own affections") appears to have only nine syllables, but *affections* is a quadri-syllable, like *conclusion* in v. 2. 41. In v. 2. 807 *lamentations* has five syllables; and the same is true of *reformation* in v. 2. 867. This lengthening occurs most frequently at the end of the line, but there are few instances of it in this play.

(*b*) Many monosyllables ending in *r*, *re*, *rs*, *res*, preceded by a long vowel or diphthong, are often made dissyllables; as *fare*, *fear*, *dear*, *fire*, *hair*, *hour* (see on ii. 1. 68), *your*, etc. If the word is repeated in a verse it is often both monosyllable and dissyllable; as in *M. of V.* iii. 2. 20: "And so, though yours, not yours. Prove it so," where either *yours* (preferably the first) is a dissyl-lable, the other being a monosyllable. In *J. C.* iii. 1. 172: "As fire drives out fire, so pity, pity," the first *fire* is a dissyllable.

(*c*) Words containing *l* or *r*, preceded by another consonant, are often pronounced as if a vowel came between or after the con-sonants; as in *T. of S.* ii. 1. 158: "While she did call me rascal fiddler" [fiddl(e)er]; *All's Well*, iii. 5. 43: "If you will tarry, holy pilgrim" [pilg(e)rim]; *C. of E.* v. 1. 360: "These are the parents of these children" (childeren, the original form of the word); *W. T.* iv. 4. 76: "Grace and remembrance [rememb(e)-rance] be to you both!" etc.

(*d*) Monosyllabic exclamations (*ay*, *O*, *yea*, *nay*, *hail*, etc.) and monosyllables otherwise emphasized are similarly lengthened; also certain longer words; as *commandement* in *M. of V.* (iv. 1. 451); *safety* (trisyllable) in *Ham.* i. 3. 21; *business* (trisyllable, as originally pronounced) in *J. C.* iv. 1. 22: "To groan and sweat under the business" (so in several other passages); and other words mentioned in the notes to the plays in which they occur. In v. 2. 334 of this play *whale's* is a dissyllable (see note).

6. Words are also *contracted* for metrical reasons, like plurals and possessives ending in a sibilant, as *balance*, *horse* (for *horses* and *horse's*), *princess*, *sense*, *marriage* (plural and possessive), *image*, etc. So with many adjectives in the superlative (like

strict'st in i. I. 117, *stern'st, kind'st, secret'st*, etc.), and certain other words.

7. The *accent* of words is also varied in many instances for metrical reasons. Thus we find both *révenue* and *revénue* in the first scene of *M. N. D.* (lines 6 and 158), *cónfine* (noun) and *confíne*, *solémnize* (see on ii. I. 42) and *sólemnize*, *cómplete* (see on i. I. 136) and *compléte*, *éxtreme* (see on v. 2. 738) and *extréme*, *pursúe* and *pursúe*, *distínct* and *dístinct*, etc.

These instances of variable accent must not be confounded with those in which words were uniformly accented differently in the time of Shakespeare; like *aspéct, impórtune, sepúlchre* (verb), *perséver* (never *persevére*), *perséverance, rheúmatic, triúmphing* (see on iv. 3. 34), etc.

8. *Alexandrines*, or verses of twelve syllables, with six accents, occur here and there in the plays. They must not be confounded with female lines with two extra syllables (see on I above) or with other lines in which two extra unaccented syllables may occur.

9. *Incomplete* verses, of one or more syllables, are scattered through the plays. See ii. I. 55, 89, 105, etc.

10. *Doggerel* measure is used in the very earliest comedies (the present play and *C. of E.* in particular) in the mouths of comic characters (and others to some extent in this play), but never anywhere in plays written after 1598.

11. *Rhyme* occurs frequently in the early plays, but diminishes with comparative regularity from that period until the latest. Thus, in this play there are about 1100 rhyming verses (more than one-third of the whole number), in *M. N. D.* about 900, in *Richard II.* and *R. and J.* about 500 each, while in *Cor.* and *A. and C.* there are only about 40 each, in *Temp.* only two, and in *W. T.* none at all, except in the chorus introducing act iv. Songs, interludes, and other matter not in ten-syllable measure (or in doggerel) are not included in this enumeration.

Alternate rhymes are found only in the plays written before 1599 or 1600. They are very frequent in the present play; as in i. I.

80–91, 100–107, 112–115, 131–138, etc. In *M. of V.* there are only four lines at the end of iii. 2. In *Much Ado* and *A. Y. L.*, we also find a few lines, but none at all in subsequent plays.

Rhymed couplets, or "rhyme-tags," are often found at the end of scenes; as in 4 of the 9 scenes of the present play. In *Ham.* 14 out of 20 scenes, and in *Macb.* 21 out of 28, have such "tags;" but in the latest plays they are not so frequent. In *Temp.*, for instance, there is but one, and in *W. T.* none.

12. In this edition of Shakespeare, the final *-ed* of past tenses and participles *in verse* is printed *-'d* when the word is to be pronounced in the ordinary way; as in *pass'd*, line 19, and *resolv'd*, line 24, of the first scene. But when the metre requires that the *-ed* be made a separate syllable, the *e* is retained; as in *enrolled*, line 38, where the word is a trisyllable. The only variation from this rule is in verbs like *cry, die, sue*, etc., the *-ed* of which is very rarely, if ever, made a separate syllable.

SHAKESPEARE'S USE OF VERSE AND PROSE IN THE PLAYS. — This is a subject to which the critics have given very little attention, but it is an interesting study. In this play we find scenes entirely in verse or in prose (except for a little doggerel), and others in which the two are mixed. In general, we may say that verse is used for what is distinctly poetical, and prose for what is not poetical. The distinction, however, is not so clearly marked in the earlier as in the later plays. The second scene of *M. of V.*, for instance, is in prose, because Portia and Nerissa are talking about the suitors in a familiar and playful way; but in *T. G. of V.*, where Julia and Lucetta are discussing the suitors of the former in much the same fashion, the scene is in verse. Dowden, commenting on *Rich. II.*, remarks: "Had Shakespeare written the play a few years later, we may be certain that the gardener and his servants (iii. 4) would not have uttered stately speeches in verse, but would have spoken homely prose, and that humour would have mingled with the pathos of the scene. The same remark may be made with reference to the subsequent scene (v. 5) in which his groom visits the dethroned king in the Tower." Comic characters and those in low life generally speak in prose in the later plays, as Dowden intimates, but in the very earliest ones doggerel verse is much used instead. See on 10 above.

The change from prose to verse is well illustrated in the third scene of *M. of V.* It begins with plain prosaic talk about a business matter; but when Antonio enters, it rises at once to the higher level of poetry. The sight of Antonio reminds Shylock of his hatred of the Merchant, and the passion expresses itself in verse, the vernacular tongue of poetry.

The reasons for the choice of prose or verse are not always so clear as in this instance. We are seldom puzzled to explain the prose, but not unfrequently we meet with verse where we might expect prose. As Professor Corson remarks (*Introduction to Shakespeare*, 1889), "Shakespeare adopted verse as the general tenor of his language, and therefore expressed much in verse that is within the capabilities of prose; in other words, his verse constantly encroaches upon the domain of prose, but his prose can never be said to encroach upon the domain of verse." If in rare instances we think we find exceptions to this latter statement, and prose actually seems to usurp the place of verse, I believe that careful study of the passage will prove the supposed exception to be apparent rather than real.

SOME BOOKS FOR TEACHERS AND STUDENTS. — A few out of the many books that might be commended to the teacher and the critical student are the following: Halliwell-Phillipps's *Outlines of the Life of Shakespeare* (7th ed. 1887); Sidney Lee's *Life of Shakespeare* (1898; for ordinary students the abridged ed. of 1899 is preferable); Rolfe's *Life of Shakespeare* (1904); Schmidt's *Shakespeare Lexicon* (3d ed. 1902); Littledale's ed. of Dyce's *Glossary* (1902); Bartlett's *Concordance to Shakespeare* (1895); Abbott's *Shakespearian Grammar* (1873); Furness's "New Variorum" ed. of *L. L. L.* (1904; encyclopædic and exhaustive); Dowden's *Shakspere: His Mind and Art* (American ed. 1881);

Hudson's *Life, Art, and Characters of Shakespeare* (revised ed. 1882); Mrs. Jameson's *Characteristics of Women* (several eds.; some with the title, *Shakespeare Heroines*); Ten Brink's *Five Lectures on Shakespeare* (1895); Boas's *Shakespeare and His Predecessors* (1895); Dyer's *Folk-lore of Shakespeare* (American ed. 1884); Gervinus's *Shakespeare Commentaries* (Bunnett's translation, 1875); Wordsworth's *Shakespeare's Knowledge of the Bible* (3d ed. 1880); Elson's *Shakespeare in Music* (1901).

Some of the above books will be useful to all readers who are interested in special subjects or in general criticism of Shakespeare. Among those which are better suited to the needs of ordinary readers and students, the following may be mentioned: Mabie's *William Shakespeare: Poet, Dramatist, and Man* (1900); Dowden's *Shakspere Primer* (1877; small but invaluable); Rolfe's *Shakespeare the Boy* (1896; not a mere juvenile book, but useful for general reference on the home and school life, the games and sports, the manners, customs, and folk-lore of the poet's time); Guerber's *Myths of Greece and Rome* (for readers and students who may need information on mythological allusions not explained in the notes).

H. Snowden Ward's *Shakespeare's Town and Times* (2d ed. 1902) and John Leyland's *Shakespeare Country* (2d ed. 1903) are copiously illustrated books (yet inexpensive) which may be particularly commended for school libraries and the general reader.

ABBREVIATIONS IN THE NOTES. — The abbreviations of the names of Shakespeare's plays will be readily understood: as *T. N.* for *Twelfth Night*, *Cor.* for *Coriolanus*, *3 Hen. VI.* for *The Third Part of King Henry the Sixth*, etc. *P. P.* refers to *The Passionate Pilgrim*; *V. and A.* to *Venus and Adonis*; *L. C.* to *Lover's Complaint*; and *Sonn.* to the *Sonnets*.

Other abbreviations that hardly need explanation are *Cf.* (*confer*, compare), *Fol.* (following), *Id.* (*idem*, the same), and *Prol.* (prologue). The numbers of the lines in the references (except for the present play) are those of the "Globe" edition (the cheapest and best edition of *Shakespeare* in one compact volume), which is now generally accepted as the standard for line-numbers in works of reference (Schmidt's *Lexicon*, Abbott's *Grammar*, Dowden's *Primer*, the publications of the New Shakspere Society, etc.).

THE TITLE OF THE PLAY. — Mason says: "I believe the title of this play should be *Love's Labours Lost*," and Dr. Furnivall agrees with him. The title-pages of the quartos give "Loues labors lost" and "Loues Labours lost;" but the running title of the quartos and 1st and 2d folios is "Loues Labour's Lost," which is clearly a contraction of "Love's Labour is Lost." In the early eds. the possessive case is commonly given without the apostrophe (as in the titles "A Midsommer nights Dreame" and "The Winters Tale"); but the contraction of *is* generally has the apostrophe (as in "All 's Well that ends Well"). Meres calls the play "Loue labors lost," and Tofte "Loues Labour Lost." I prefer (with the great majority of editors) to follow the folio rather than the quarto, which is not consistent with itself.

In the quartos the play is not divided into acts or scenes. In the folio it is divided into acts of very unequal length, "the first being half as long again, the fourth twice as long, the fifth three times as long, as the second and third" (Spedding).

DRAMATIS PERSONÆ. — In the quartos and the folio no list of *dramatis personæ* is given. *Biron* is spelt "Berowne," and in iv. 3. 230 it rhymes with "moon." *Mercade* appears as "Marcade" in the quartos and 1st folio, and *Armado* is sometimes "Armatho." White thinks that *Moth* should be printed "Mote," as it was clearly so pronounced. In some other words *th* was pronounced like *t*. Hence the pun on *Goths* and *goats* in *A. Y. L.* iii. 3. 9, etc. In *Sonn.* 20 we find *nothing* rhyming with *doting*. In i. 2. 90 of the present play, in "She had a green wit" some critics see an allusion to the "green withes" used in binding Samson. *Boyet* rhymes with *debt* in v. 2. 336; *Longaville* with *ill* in iv. 3. 118, and with *mile* in v. 2. 53; and *Rosaline* with *thine* in iv. 3. 220. Costard, in the old stage-directions, is called "Clown."

COSTUME. — As Knight remarks, Cesare Vecellio, in his *Habiti Antichi* (ed. 1598), gives us the general costume of Navarre at this period. We are told that some dressed in imitation of the French, and some in the style of the Spaniards, while others blended the fashions of both these nations. The cut on p. 9 is from Vecellio, and shows the Spanish gentleman and the French lady of 1589. For the costume of the Muscovites in the masque, see on v. 2. 121 below, and cf. cut on p. 147.

ACT I

SCENE I. — 3. *Disgrace.* Disfigurement; as in *Sonn.* 33. 8, where it refers to the clouded sun.

6. *Bate.* Blunt; not to be printed "'bate," as by some editors. Cf. *bateless* in *R. of L.* 9: "bateless edge;" and *unbated* in *Ham.* iv. 7. 139: "A sword unbated;" and *Id.* v. 2. 328: "Unbated and envenom'd."

9. *Affections.* A quadrisyllable here.

11. *Edict.* Accented by S. on either syllable, as suits the measure. Cf. the present instance and *M. N. D.* i. 1. 151 with *Rich. III.* i. 4. 203, etc.

13. *Academe.* Academy; used by S. only here and in iv. 3. 301 and 350 below.

14. *Living art.* "Immortal science" (Schmidt). For *art* = letters, learning in general, cf. iv. 2. 113 below.

23. *Deep oaths.* For the use of *deep*, cf. *Sonn.* 152. 9: "I have sworn deep oaths;" *R. of L.* 1847: "that deep vow;" and *K. John*, iii. 1. 231: "deep-sworn faith." For the use of *it* apparently referring to *oaths*, Dyce compares 1 *Hen. VI.* i. 1. 165: "I do remember 't;" that is, "your oaths to Henry" in the pre-

ceding speech. In both cases *it* may be = what I have sworn. See also *Two Noble Kinsmen*, i. 1 : —

> " You cannot read *it* there ; there, through my tears,
> Like wrinkled pebbles in a glassy stream,
> You may behold '*em*."

27. *Bankrupt quite.* The 1st quarto has " bancrout quite," the folios only " bankerout." The word is often thus spelt (or similarly, as " bankrout," etc.) in the early eds. and other books of the time.

29. *These world's delights.* These worldly delights.

32. *All these.* Johnson is probably right in making *these* refer to *love, wealth,* and *pomp;* not, as some suppose, to the speaker's companions. Dumain dies to these worldly delights, only to find them living in philosophy. Mr. P. A. Daniel conjectures " all three."

43. *Wink.* Shut the eyes ; as often in S. Cf. *Sonn.* 43. 1, 56. 6, *Temp.* ii. 1. 216, *C. of E.* iii. 2. 58, etc. For *of* = during, cf. *T. of S.* ind. 2. 84 : " But did I never speak of all that time ? "

50. *An if.* Often, like *and if*, used for *if*.

54. *By yea and nay.* Cf. "by yea and no" in *M. W.* iv. 2. 202, etc.

62. *Feast.* The quartos and folios all have "fast ;" corrected by Theobald. He suggested as an alternative " fore-bid " (= "enjoined beforehand ") for *forbid;* but S. never uses that word.

64. *From common sense.* That is, from ordinary sight or perception. Cf. " the sense of sense " (= the sight of the eye) in v. 2. 260 below.

65. *Too hard a keeping oath.* For the transposition of the article, cf. *K. John,* iv. 2. 27 : " So new a fashion'd robe ; " *C. of E.* iii. 2. 186 : " so fair an offer'd chain ; " *T. and C.* v. 6. 20 : " much more a fresher man," etc.

77. *Light seeking light,* etc. Furness would point " Light-seeking light," making this the subject of *doth.* He explains the passage correctly : " The eyes which are seeking for truth deprive themselves (by too much application) of the power of seeing." But this is the meaning with the ordinary pointing. The first *Light* can refer to the eyes as he makes the third *light* ("themselves" referring to "eyes"), and it seems to me simpler to explain it so.

80. *Study me.* The *me* is the expletive pronoun, or "ethical dative," often used, as here, with a slight dash of humour.

82. *Who dazzling so,* etc. "That when he *dazzles*, that is, has his eye made weak, by fixing his eye upon a fairer eye, that *fairer* eye shall be his *heed*, his *direction* or *lodestar*, and give him light that was blinded by it" (Johnson). Schmidt defines *heed* here as = "guard, protection, means of safety." Furness paraphrases the passage well: "A woman's eye, by its dangerous beauty, will compel the gazer to take heed, and thereby, in effect, restore to him the light whereof he had been deprived."

87. *Base.* Perhaps, as Walker conjectures, a misprint for "bare." Marshall takes it to be figuratively = "base-born" (as in *Lear*, i. 2. 10), and paraphrases the passage thus: "Continual plodders discover nothing new, but only learn to take other persons' opinions as their own."

91. *Wot.* Know; used only in the present and the participle *wotting*, for which see *W. T.* iii. 2. 77.

92. *Too much to know,* etc. "The consequence, says Biron, of too much knowledge, is not any real solution of doubts, but mere reputation; that is, too much knowledge gives only *fame*, a name which every godfather can give likewise" (Johnson); or, as Clarke puts it: "To know overmuch is not to be wise, but to get the name of being wise: and every godfather (like *these earthly godfathers* that name the stars) can give a man a name for wisdom."

95. *Proceeded well,* etc. There is a play upon *proceed*, which, as Johnson notes, is "an academical term, meaning to take a degree, as *he proceeded bachelor in physic*."

100. *Sneaping.* Snipping, or nipping. Cf. *W. T.* i. 2. 13: "sneaping winds;" and *R. of L.* 333: "the sneaped birds." For the noun *sneap* (= snubbing) see *2 Hen. IV.* ii. 1. 133: "I will not undergo this sneap without reply."

106. *Shows*. The early eds. have "showes" or "shows." Theobald substituted "earth" for the sake of the rhyme, and some read "mirth" (the conjecture of Walker). Malone thinks that a line rhyming with 104 may have been lost; but lines without rhyme are sometimes found in rhymed passages. *Fangled* in *Cymb*. v. 4. 134 (the only instance in S.) means *gaudy*; and *new-fangled shows* may mean "May's first gaudy shows of flowers."

107. *Like of*. Cf. *Much Ado*, v. 4. 59: "I am your husband, if you like of me." See also iv. 3. 156 below.

108. *So you, to study*, etc. This is the quarto reading, and is generally adopted, though there may be some corruption. The folio has: —

> "So you to studie now it is too late,
> That were to clymbe ore the house to vnlocke the gate."

White reads: —

> "So you to study now; — it is too late:
> That were to climb the house o'er to unlock the gate;"

which he explains thus: "Birone, in justification of his ridicule of these literary pursuits, says that they are untimely, that he likes not roses at Christmas or snow in May, and adds, 'So it is too late for you to study now: that were to climb over a house to unlock a gate;' or, in other words, 'you are beginning at the wrong end — doing boys' work at men's years.' But, according to the quarto, he says, 'I like of each thing that in season grows; *so* you, now it is too late to study, climb o'er the house to unlock the little gate:' whereas it was not *so* (that is, like Birone) at all, but exactly *not* so." I take it, however, that *to study now it is too late* is = in studying now that it is too late; the infinitive being used in the "indefinite" way, so common in S. The general meaning of the passage seems to be: "Things done out of season are commonly done by laborious and indirect processes" (Herford). If the folio is to be followed, it is better to take it just as it is, making it a line of five feet with slurred syllables, than to turn it into an

alexandrine, as White does. Alexandrines are extremely rare in
the early plays of S. Mr. Fleay (Dr. Ingleby's *S. the Man and the
Book*, Part II. p. 71) finds only four in *L. L. L.*, one of which is
doubtful.

110. *Sit you out.* The expression is one used in card-playing
for taking no part in the game.

112. *Barbarism.* Ignorance, neglect of *knowledge*, or learning.

114. *Swore.* The reading of the later folios, and required by
the rhyme. The quartos and 1st folio have "sworne." Elsewhere
S. has *sworn* for the participle, but we find *broke* for *broken*, *froze*
for *frozen*, *smote* for *smitten*, etc. Cf. *forgot* in 141 below, and
chose in 169.

128. *Gentility!* Refinement, courtesy. In the only other instance
of the word in S. (*A. Y. L.* i. 1. 22) it is = gentle birth. The early
eds. make the line a part of Longaville's speech ; but Theobald is
clearly right in transferring it to Biron.

136. *Complete.* Accented on the first syllable because preceding
a noun so accented. Cf. *prófound* in iv. 3. 166, and *éxtreme* in v.
2. 738.

140–142. *So study*, etc. "These lines form a most excellent vindi-
cation of the opinions uttered before by Biron. The *study* here is that
exaggerated habit of studious industry which neglects, for labours
excessive but comparatively useless, the wholesome work of everyday life. He also points out the absurdity of retiring from the
world, as the King proposed, imposing unnecessary duties on themselves while neglecting those necessary to their station" (Marshall).

147. *Of force.* Perforce, of necessity ; as in *M. N. D.* iii. 2. 40,
M. of V. iv. 1. 56, 421, etc.

148. *Lie.* Lodge, reside. Reed quotes Wotton's definition :
"An ambassador is an honest man sent to lie abroad for the good
of his country." Cf. *M. W.* ii. 1. 187 : "Does he lie at the Garter?"
etc. *Mere* = absolute ; as often. Cf. i. 2. 33 below.

151. *Affects.* Affections, or passions ; as in *Rich. II.* i. 4. 30
and *Oth.* i. 3. 264.

158. *Suggestions.* Temptations ; the usual meaning in S. Cf. the verb in v. 2. 768 below.

160. *I am the last that will last keep his oath.* Changes have been suggested, on the ground that Biron is made to say the contrary of what he means ; but S. sometimes twists the sense of a word a little for the sake of a repetition like this.

161. *Quick.* Lively, animated ; as in i. 2. 23, 29, v. 1. 59, and v. 2. 284 below. Cf. its use = living ; for which see *Ham.* v. 1. 137, 274, 302, etc.; also *Acts*, x. 42, etc.

166. *One whom.* The 1st folio has "One who," which might be retained. Cf. iv. 1. 72 below.

168. *Complements.* Probably = accomplishments, as Johnson and others explain it. Schmidt takes it to be = external show. The early eds. make no distinction between *complement* and *compliment.*

170. *Hight.* Is called ; used by S. only as an archaism. Cf. 255 below. See also *M. N. D.* v. 1. 140 and *Per.* iv. prol. 18.

173. *Debate.* Contest, quarrel ; the only sense in S. Cf. *M. N. D.* ii. 1. 116, 2 *Hen. IV.* iv. 4. 2, etc.

176. *I will use him for my minstrelsy.* "I will make a *minstrel* of him, whose occupation was to relate fabulous stories" (Douce).

178. *Fire-new.* Brand-new, fresh from the mint. Cf. *Rich. III.* i. 3. 256 : "Your fire-new stamp of honour is scarce current ; " *T. N.* iii. 2. 23 : "fire-new from the mint," etc. Furness suggests that S. may have coined the compound, as no earlier example of it than that in *Rich. III.* has been noted.

181. *Duke's.* Changed by Theobald to "King's ; " but cf. i. 2. 36 and 128 below, where Armado uses it in the same blundering way. We find it even in the mouth of the princess in ii. 1. 38. Dogberry applies the word to the prince in *Much Ado*, iii. 5. 22.

184. *Tharborough.* For *thirdborough*, a kind of constable, for whom see *T. of S.* ind. 1. 12.

190. *Contempts.* Contents, of course.

195. *Having.* Possession. The early eds. have "heaven,"

which the Cambridge editors and a few others retain. Staunton remarks: "The allusion may be to the representations of *heaven*, and the attendant personifications of Faith, *Hope*, etc., in the ancient pageants." For *having*, cf. *A. Y. L.* iii. 2. 396: "Your having in beard," etc.

197. *Laughing.* The early eds. have "hearing;" corrected by Capell. The old reading has been defended, and Furness would retain it.

200. *Style.* There is an evident play on *stile;* as in iv. 1. 95 below. See also *Much Ado*, v. 2. 6.

203. *Taken with the manner.* A law term = taken in the fact, or in the act. Cf. 1 *Hen. IV.* ii. 4. 347 and *W. T.* iv. 4. 752. Halliwell-Phillipps quotes *Termes de la Ley:* "Maynour is when a theefe hath stolne, and is followed with Hue and Cry, and taken, having that found upon him which he stole, that is called Maynour. And so we use to say when we find one doing of an unlawful act, that we took him with the Maynour or Manner."

206. *Form.* Bench. For the play upon the word, cf. *R. and J.* ii. 4. 36: "who stand so much on the new form that they cannot sit at ease on the old bench."

226. *But so.* Equivalent to "but so-so," which Hanmer substituted.

240. *Ycleped.* Called; an archaism put only into the mouths of Armado and Holofernes. Cf. v. 2. 599 below.

246. *Curious-knotted.* Elaborately laid out in *knots*, or interlacing beds; a technical term. Cf. *Rich. II.* iii. 4. 46: "Her knots disorder'd;" and Milton, *P. L.* iv. 242: "In beds and curious knots." See the cut on p. 8.

253. *Vassal.* Possibly there is a play on *vessel*.

258. *Sorted.* Associated; as in 2 *Hen. IV.* ii. 4. 162 and *Ham.* ii. 2. 274. Cf. Bacon, *Essay* 7: "Makes them sort with meane Company."

259. *Continent canon.* Law concerning continence.

260. *Passion.* Sorrow, grieve. Cf. *T. G. of V.* iv. 4. 172:

"Ariadne passioning For Theseus' perjury;" and *V. and A.*
1059: "Dumbly she passions, franticly she doteth." Cf. the noun
in v. 2. 118 below.

271. *The weaker vessel.* Taken from 1 *Peter,* iii. 7 (cf. *A. Y. L.*
ii. 4. 6, 2 *Hen. IV.* ii. 4. 66, and *R. and J.* i. i. 20), as *vessel of thy
law's fury* from *Romans,* ix. 22.

287. *Damosel.* The folio has "damosell" here and in the next
two lines, the 1st quarto "damsel." Holofernes makes it "damosella" in iv. 2. 130 below.

305. *Lay.* Stake, wager. Cf. *Hen. V.* iv. 1. 242: "lay twenty
French crowns to one," etc.

SCENE II. — 5. *Imp.* Youngling; used only by Armado, Holofernes, and Pistol. The word originally meant an offshoot or scion
of a tree; thence, figuratively, offspring or child; finally becoming
limited to a young devil. Johnson remarks that Lord Cromwell,
in his last letter to Henry VIII., prays for *the imp his son.* Spenser
in the prologue to *F. Q.* addresses Cupid as

> "most dreaded impe of highest Jove,
>   Faire Venus sonne."

Cf. *F. Q.* iii. 5. 53 : —

> "Fayre ympes of beauty, whose bright shining beames
>   Adorne the world with like to heavenly light," etc.

6. *O Lord, sir.* This expression was much in vogue at court
and in society in the time of S., and the Clown in *A. W.* ii. 2
makes fun of it.

8. *Juvenal.* Juvenile, youth; used only by Armado, Flute
(*M. N. D.* iii. 1. 97), and in jest by Falstaff (2 *Hen. IV.* i. 2. 22).

11. *Senior.* The 1st quarto has "signeor," and the 1st folio
"signeur." See footnote on p. 16 above.

14. *Epitheton.* Epithet; the reading of 2d folio. The 1st folio
has "apathaton," and the quarto "apethaton."

34. *Crosses love not him.* The boy plays on *crosses* as applied

to coin, on account of the cross stamped on them. We have the same pun in *A. Y. L.* ii. 4. 12 and *2 Hen. IV.* i. 2. 253. *Mere =* absolute, very. See on i. 1. 148 above.

41. *A tapster.* For other allusions to the tapster's dishonest *reckoning,* or keeping account with customers, cf. *2 Hen. IV.* i. 2. 193 and *T. and C.* i. 2. 123.

44. *Complete.* Accomplished. Cf. *Hen. VIII.* i. 2. 118: "This man so complete," etc.

53. *The dancing horse.* A famous horse of the time, often called "Bankes' horse" from his owner, who had trained him to perform many remarkable feats. Raleigh, in his *Hist. of the World,* says: "If Banks had lived in older times, he would have shamed all the inchanters in the world; for whosoever was most famous among them could never master or instruct any beast as he did his horse." Steevens quotes, among other allusions to the animal, Jonson, *Every Man Out of His Humour :* "He keeps more ado with this monster than ever Bankes did with his horse ; " and the same author's *Epigrams : —*

> "Old Banks the jugler, our Pythagoras,
> Grave tutor to the learned horse."

In France, according to Bishop Morton, Bankes "was brought into suspition of magicke, because of the strange feates which his horse Morocco plaied at Orleance ; " but Bankes having made the beast kneel down to a crucifix and kiss it, "his adversaries rested satisfied, conceiving (as it might seeme) that the divell had no power to come neare the crosse." In Rome he was less fortunate, if we may believe Reed, who says that both horse and owner were there burned by order of the Pope. According to other authorities, however, Bankes came back safe to London, and was still living in King Charles's time, a jolly vintner in Cheapside. For fuller accounts of him and his horse, see Douce's *Illustrations,* Chambers's *Book of Days,* or Halliwell-Phillipps's folio ed.

63. *Courtesy.* Curtsy; used by men as well as women. Cf.

Rich. III. i. 3. 49: "Duck with French nods and apish courtesy;"
A. W. v. 3. 324: "Let thy courtesies alone; they are scurvy ones,"
etc.

68. *Sweet my child.* My sweet child. Cf. "dear my lord," etc.

83. *The four complexions.* Those connected with the four
humours — "the sanguine, phlegmatic, choleric, and melancholy."

86. *Green indeed is the colour of lovers.* Some say, because of
its association with jealousy, "the green-eyed monster;" others,
as being the colour of the *willow*, "worn of forlorn paramours,"
for which, see *M. of V.* v. 1. 10, *Oth.* iv. 3. 28 fol., v. 2. 248, etc.

90. *A green wit.* Possibly, as the Cambridge editors remark,
there is an allusion to the *green withes* with which Samson was
bound. See p. 154 above (on DRAMATIS PERSONÆ). It is doubtful, however, whether *withe* was ever pronounced *wit.*

93. *Maculate.* The reading of the 1st quarto; the other early
eds. have "immaculate."

107. *Native she doth owe.* She possesses by nature. For *owe*
= own, cf. ii. 1. 6 below.

110. *The King and the Beggar.* The ballad of *King Cophetua
and the Beggar-maid*, which may be found in Percy's *Reliques*.
For other allusions to it, see iv. 1. 65 below, *R. and J.* ii. 1. 14
and *Rich. II.* v. 3. 80.

117. *Digression.* Going out of the right way, transgression.
Cf. *R. of L.* 202 : —

> "Then my digression is so vile, so base,
> That it will live engraven in my face."

Cf. also *digressing* in *Rich. II.* v. 3. 66.

119. *Rational hind.* Perhaps Armado's fantastic way of expressing "human hind," *hind* being a beast (a deer), as well as a boor;
or = "reasoning beast" (Marshall). Farmer objects to this interpretation that it makes Costard a *female* animal; but Steevens
quotes in reply *J. C.* i. 3. 106: "He were no lion, were not

omans hinds." The meaning may be, as Furness suggests, that ostard, though a peasant, is no fool.

124. *A light wench.* S. is fond of playing upon the different nses of *light.* Cf. *M. of V.* v. 1. 130 : —

> " Let me give light, but let me not be light ;
> For a light wife doth make a heavy husband."

ee also ii. 1. 199 and v. 2. 25 below ; and for *light* = wanton, iv. 383.

132. *Day-woman.* Dairy-woman. *Dey* or *deye* was an old rm for such a servant ; and still current, in a more general nse, in Scotland (*New Eng. Dict.*).

136. *That's hereby.* "*Hereby* is used by her (as among the ulgar in some countries) to signify *as it may happen;* he takes it the sense of *just by*" (Steevens). We have it in the latter sense iv. 1. 9 below, but it is doubtful whether it ever had the former ne. The only other instance of the word in S. is in *Rich. III.* 4. 94.

137. *Situate.* For the form, Cf. *C. of E.* ii. 1. 16.

140. *With that face?* Steevens says : "This cant phrase has ddly lasted till the present time ; and is used by people who have o more meaning annexed to it than Fielding had, who, putting it to the mouth of Beau Didapper, thinks it necessary to apologize in a note) for its want of sense, by adding that ' it was taken ver- atim from very polite conversation.'" The 1st folio has "what ace," which Furness defends (= what effrontery, or presumption).

145. *Come, Jaquenetta, away!* Given by the quartos and the lio to " *Clo.*" (that is, *Clown,* or Costard) ; corrected by Theobald. he next speech is given by the 1st quarto to "*Ar.,*" by the 1st lio to "*Clo.,*" and by the later folios to "*Con.*"

157. *Fast and loose.* A quibbling reference to the cheating ame so called. Cf. iii. 1. 104 below. See also *K. John,* iii. 1. 242 nd *A. and C.* iv. 12. 28.

167. *Affect.* Love; as in 88 above. Cf. *Much Ado*, i. 1. 298: "Dost thou affect her?" etc.

170. *Argument.* Proof; as in *Much Ado*, ii. 3. 243, *T. N.* iii. 2. 12, etc.

172. *Familiar.* "Familiar spirit," or demon; as in 2 *Hen. VI.* iv. 7. 114: "he has a familiar under his tongue," etc. Cf. also the adjective in *Sonn.* 86. 9: —

> "that affable familiar ghost
> Which nightly gulls him with intelligence."

176. *Butt-shaft.* A kind of arrow used for shooting at *butts*, or targets. Cf. *R. and J.* ii. 4. 16.

178. *The first and second cause*, etc. Alluding to the classified *causes of quarrel* in the elaborate duelling science of the time. Cf. Touchstone's ridicule of them in *A. Y. L.* v. 4. 52 fol. As Saviolo's book, evidently alluded to here, was printed in 1594, this passage is one of the indications of the revision of the play before the publication of the 1st quarto.

179. *Passado.* A thrust in fencing. See *R. and J.* ii. 4. 26, iii. 1. 18, etc. *Duello* occurs again in *T. N.* iii. 4. 337.

182. *Manager.* The verb *manage* is often used of *arms*. Cf. *Rich. II.* iii. 2. 118, 2 *Hen. IV.* iii. 2. 292, 301, *R. and J.* i. 1. 76, etc.

184. *Sonnet.* The reading of all the early eds. changed by some to "sonneteer," "sonneter," or "sonnetist." *Turn sonnet* is not unlike Armado. Cf. *Much Ado*, ii. 3. 21: "now is he turned orthography;" where some read "orthographer" or "orthographist."

ACT II

SCENE I. — 1. *Dearest.* Best, highest. Cf. iv. 1. 85 below. See also "dearest speed" (1 *Hen. IV.* v. 5. 36), etc.

2. *Who.* For *whom;* as often. It is sometimes used even after prepositions; as in "To who?" (*Cymb.* iv. 2. 75, *Oth.* i. 2.

52), "With who?" (*Oth.* iv. 2. 99), etc. In the next line here *whom* is used correctly.

5. *Inheritor.* Possessor; as in *Rich. III.* iv. 3. 34, and *Ham.* v. 1. 121.

6. *Owe.* See on i. 2. 107 above.

7. *Plea.* Claim, suit.

16. *Chapmen.* Here = sellers; but usually = buyers, as in *T. and C.* iv. 1. 75. Johnson remarks: "*cheap* or *cheaping* was anciently the *market*; *chapman* therefore is *marketman*." *Utter'd* is here used in the commercial sense of "made to pass from one hand to another." Cf. *R. and J.* v. 1. 67, *W. T.* iv. 4. 330, etc. The meaning of the passage is that the estimation of beauty depends not on the tongue of the seller, but on the eye of the buyer. Cf. *Sonn.* 102. 4 : —

> "That love is merchandiz'd whose rich esteeming
> The owner's tongue doth publish everywhere."

23. *Painful.* Painstaking, exacting.

25. *To 's seemeth.* Cf. *W. T.* iv. 4. 65: "friends to 's welcome," etc. Such contractions of *us* occur often in the latest plays, but seldom in the early ones.

28. *Bold of.* Confident of, trusting in.

29. *Best-moving.* Most eloquent.

32. *Importunes.* Accented on the penult by S.

42. *Jaques.* Always a dissyllable in S. *Solemnized* is here accented on the second syllable; but on the first in *M. of V.* ii. 9. 6 and iii. 2. 194. Furness says the word has "two accents here;" but no more so than *Longaville* in the next line, or any word coming under the rule (4) on p. 148 above.

45. *Well fitted in the arts.* "*Well fitted* is *well qualified*" (Johnson).

49. *Blunt.* "Too dull in regard to the feeling of others" (Furness).

57. *Of all.* That is, by all; a common use of *of.*

62. *And much too little,* etc. "And my report of the good I saw is much too little *compared* to his great worthiness" (Heath).

68. *Hour's.* A dissyllable ; as often.

72. *Conceit's expositor.* The exponent of his thought ; a very common meaning of *conceit.*

82. *Competitors.* Associates, partners. Cf. *T. N.* iv. 2. 12, or *A. and C.* ii. 7. 76, v. 1. 42, etc.

83. *Address'd.* Prepared, ready. Cf. *J. C.* iii. 1. 29, *Hen. V.* iii. 3. 58, etc.

88. *Unpeopled.* The Cambridge editors strangely prefer the quarto "unpeeled," which they (like Schmidt) take to be = "stripped, desolate," though (as *peel* is = strip) it ought to have the opposite meaning.

90. *Welcome to the court,* etc. The king gives the usual formal welcome to his guests ; but the Princess mischievously criticizes his use of *court.*

103. *Where.* Whereas ; as often. Cf. *Lear,* i. 2. 89, *Cor.* i. 1. 102, i. 10. 12, etc.

106. *And sin to break it.* Hanmer changes *And* to "Not ; " but, as Johnson remarks, "the princess shows an inconvenience very frequently attending rash oaths, which, whether kept or broken, produce guilt."

110. *Resolve.* Answer. Cf. *T. of S.* iv. 2. 7 : "What, master, read you? First resolve me that," etc. *Suddenly* = quickly, promptly.

119. *Long of.* Owing to, because of ; as in *M. N. D.* iii. 2. 339 : "all this coil is long of you," etc. It is generally printed "'long of" in the modern eds., but not in the early ones. *Along of* in this sense does not occur in S.

124. *Fair befall,* etc. Cf. *Rich. III.* i. 3. 282 : "Now fair befall thee and thy noble house ! " etc. *Fair fall* in the next line is used in the same sense ; as in *K. John,* i. 1. 78, etc.

131. *Being but the one half,* etc. Cf. the reference to Monstrelet's *Chronicles,* p. 16 above.

147. *Depart.* Part. Cf. *K. John,* ii. 1. 563: "Hath willingly departed with a part."

149. *Gelded.* Maimed; a favourite figure with S., as Steevens notes. Cf. *W. T.* iv. 4. 623, *Rich. II.* ii. 1. 237, 1 *Hen. IV.* iii. 1. 110, etc.

174. *As you.* That you; as not unfrequently after *so.*

190. *No point.* A play on the French negative *point;* as in v. 2. 278 below. *No point* was sometimes used as an emphatic negative. Steevens quotes *The Shoemaker's Holiday,* 1600: "No point. Shall I betray my brother?"

195. *Katherine.* The early eds. have "Rosaline" here, and "Katharine" for *Rosaline* in 210 below. They confuse the names of characters in other places also.

199. *Light in the light.* See on i. 2. 124 above.

203. *God's blessing on your beard!* "That is, mayst thou have sense and seriousness more proportionate to thy beard, the length of which suits ill with such idle catches of wit!" (Johnson).

218. *Grapple.* Like *board,* a figure taken from naval warfare. The play on *ships* and *sheeps* indicates that the words were pronounced nearly alike. We find the same quibble in *C. of E.* iv. 1. 93 and *T. G. of V.* i. 1. 73.

223. *Though several they be.* A play on *several,* which meant an enclosed field in distinction from a *common.* Steevens quotes, among other examples of the word, Holinshed, *Hist. of England:* "not to take and pale in the commons, to enlarge their severalls." *Though* seems used somewhat peculiarly, and has been explained as = *since.* Staunton's explanation is better: "If we take both as places devoted to pasture — the one for general, the other for particular use — the meaning is easy enough. Boyet asks permission to graze on her lips. 'Not so,' she answers; 'my lips, though intended for the purpose, are not for general use.'" It occurs to me that there may be a play on *several* = separate; that is, there are two of them.

234. *Retire.* For the noun, cf. *K. John,* ii. 1. 326, v. 5. 4, etc.

235. *Thorough.* Used by S. interchangeably with *through.*

236. *Like an agate.* For the figures cut in agates, cf. *Much Ado,* iii. 1. 65: "an agate very vilely cut."

238. *All impatient to speak and not see,* etc. "If we take *not see* to imply 'not see, because it is not the tongue's faculty to see,' the sentence means that his tongue hurried to his eyes that it might express what they beheld" (Clarke). A writer in the *Edin. Mag.* (Nov. 1786) explains it: "his tongue envied the quickness of his eyes, and strove to be as rapid in his utterance as they in their perception." Perhaps Johnson is right in making it = "being impatiently desirous to see as well as speak." Dyce paraphrases it thus: "His tongue, not able to endure the having merely the power of speaking without that of seeing;" or vexed at not being able to see as well as speak. I think that this is the meaning.

241. *To feel only looking.* Apparently = to have no perception but that of looking, to have their own sense transformed to that of sight.

245. *Point you.* Direct you, suggest to you.

246. *Margent.* Alluding to the practice of putting notes, etc., in the margin of books. Cf. *R. and J.* i. 3. 86: —

> "And what obscur'd in this fair volume lies
> Find written in the margent of his eyes;"

Ham. v. 2. 162: "edified by the margent," etc.

250. *Dispos'd.* "Inclined to merriment" (Schmidt); "inclined to rather loose mirth, somewhat wantonly merry" (Dyce). Schmidt gives the word the same sense in v. 2. 468 below, and in *T. N.* ii. 3. 88. Boyet parries the reproof by taking the word in its ordinary meaning.

ACT III

SCENE I. — 1. *Passionate.* Referring to "the lover's luxury of woe." "A plaintive love-song was sometimes called a *passion*," as Furness shows by apt quotations.

2. *Concolinel.* Evidently a scrap of a song, but whether the beginning or the burden of it, the title or the tune, it is impossible to determine. The songs in the old plays were often omitted in the manuscripts and printed copies, being indicated, as here, by some abbreviation, or merely by a stage-direction, as "*Here they sing*" or the Latin "*Cantant.*"

5. *Festinately.* Hastily, quickly. Cf. *festinate* in *Lear*, iii. 7. 10.

8. *Brawl.* A kind of dance (Fr. *branle*). "It was performed by several persons uniting hands in a circle and giving each other continual shakes, the steps changing with the time" (Douce). Steevens quotes Jonson, *Time Vindicated :* —

> "The Graces did them footing teach ;
> And, at the old Idalian brawls,
> They danc'd your mother down."

11. *Canary to it.* The *canary* was a lively dance ; sometimes, like certain other old dances, accompanied by a song. See Elson (*S. and Music*, p. 139). Cf. *A. W.* ii. 1. 77 : —

> "make you dance canary
> With spritely fire and motion."

13. *Sometime.* Used by S. interchangeably with *sometimes.*

16. *Penthouse-like.* Like a *penthouse*, a porch with a sloping roof, common in the domestic architecture of the time of S. There was one on the house in which tradition says he was born. The cut on the following page is copied from an old print. For *penthouse*, cf. *Much Ado*, iii. 3. 110 and *M. of V.* ii. 6. 1.

17. *Thin-belly doublet.* Many of the modern eds. have "thin belly-doublet ; " but the 1st quarto reads "thinbellies" and the folios "thinbellie," or (2d folio) "thinebelly." Cf. the description of the thick-bellied doublets in Stubbes's *Anatomie of Abuses*, 1583 : "Their dublettes are noe lesse monstrous than the reste ; For now the fashion is to haue them hang downe to the middest of their theighes . . . beeing so harde-quilted, and stuffed, bombasted and sewed, as they can verie hardly eyther stoupe downe, or decline

them selues to the grounde, soe styffe and sturdy they stand about them. . . .   Now, what handsomnes can be in these dubblettes whiche stand on their bellies like, . . . (so as their bellies are thicker than all their bodyes besyde) let wise men iudge ; For for my parte, handsomnes in them I see none, and muche lesse profyte. . . .   Certaine I am there was neuer any kinde of apparell euer inuented that could more disproportion the body of man than these Dublets with great bellies, . . . stuffed with foure, fiue or six pound of Bombast at the least." For *bombast*, as here used, see on v. 2. 779 below.

JOHN SHAKESPEARE'S HOUSE IN HENLEY STREET

19. *After the old painting.*   "It was a common trick among some of the most indolent of the ancient masters, to place the hands in the bosom or the pockets, or conceal them in some other part of the drapery, to avoid the labour of representing them, or to disguise their own want of skill to employ them with grace and propriety" (Steevens) ; but this practice may not be referred to here.

21. *Complements.*   Accomplishments.   See on i. 1. 168 above.

22. *Nice.*   Coy ; as in v. 2. 220 below.

27. *By my penny of observation.*   Probably alluding to the famous old piece called *A Penniworth of Wit* (Farmer).

29. *The hobby-horse is forgot.*   Moth follows up the " But O, but

O—" with the remainder of a line in an old song bewailing the omission of the hobby-horse from the May games. Cf. *Ham.* iii. 2. 142 : "or else shall he suffer not thinking on, with the hobby-horse, whose epitaph is ' For, O, for, O, the hobby-horse is forgot ! ' " See also Jonson, *Entertainment at Althorpe :* " But see, the hobby-horse is forgot ; " Beaumont and Fletcher, *Women Pleased*, iv. 1 : " Shall the hobby-horse be forgot then ? " etc. This omission is said to have been due to the opposition made by the Puritans to the morris-dances of the May festivities. For an account of these games, see Brand's *Popular Antiquities* or my *Shakespeare the Boy*. The *hobby-horse*, says Tollet, " is a spirited horse of pasteboard, in which the master dances and displays tricks of legerdemain." A dish was hung from the horse's mouth for receiving money given by the lookers-on. *Hobby-horse* was also a term of contempt for a harlot ; as the next speech suggests. Cf. *W. T.* i. 2. 276 and *Oth.* iv. 1. 160.

51. *Message.* The meaning seems to be that the foolish message is *well sympathized* (or has its appropriate counterpart) in the foolish messenger.

53. *Ha, ha !* Probably not expressing laughter, but = " Hey ? hey ? " as Furness suggests, comparing *M. of V.* ii. 5. 46.

57. *Swift.* Quick at repartee. Cf. *T. of S.* v. 2. 54 : " A good swift simile," etc.

66. *Voluble.* The folio reading ; the 1st quarto has " volable," which the Cambridge ed. retains, as = nimble, quick.

67. *By thy favour*, etc. " *Welkin* is the sky, to which Armado, with the false dignity of a Spaniard, makes an apology for sighing in its face " (Johnson).

70. *A costard broken*, etc. He plays on the word *costard*, which was used jocosely for head. Cf. *Rich. III.* i. 4. 159, *Lear*, iv. 6. 247, etc.

72. *No salve in them all.* The early eds. have " in thee male " or " in the male." Johnson conjectured " in the mail " (that is, in the *bag*), which is very plausible, as *mail* (or *male*) was often used

in that sense. The word *mail* is not used by S., except in *T. and C.* iii. 3. 52, where it is = armour. As Clarke says, Costard seems to take *enigma*, *riddle*, and *l'envoy* to be various kinds of salve. On the virtue of the *plantain* for a *broken shin*, cf. *R. and J.* i. 2. 52 :

> " *Romeo.* Your plantain-leaf is excellent for that.
> *Benvolio.* For what, I pray thee ?
> *Romeo.*   For your broken shin."

Broken, by the way, means bruised so as to be bloody, not fractured, as some have supposed.

77. *Spleen.* For the association with laughter, cf. v. 2. 117 below.

81. *Is not l'envoy a salve?* Some see here a pun on *salve* and the Latin *salve*, which was used sometimes as a *parting* salutation ; but this is improbable.

84. *Tofore.* Cf. *T. A.* iii. 1. 294 : "as thou tofore hast been." *Sain* is Armado's rhyming " license " for *said*.

102. *The boy hath sold him a bargain.* "This comedy is running over with allusions to country sports — one of the many proofs that, in its original shape, it may be assigned to the author's greenest years. The sport which so delights Costard, about the fox, the ape, and the humble-bee, has been explained by Capell, whose lumbering and obscure comments upon Shakespeare have been pillaged and sneered at by the other commentators. In this instance, they take no notice of him. It seems, according to Capell, that 'selling a bargain' consisted in drawing a person in, by some stratagem, to proclaim himself fool, by his own lips ; and thus, when Moth makes his master repeat the *l'envoy*, ending in the goose, he proclaims himself a goose, according to the rustic wit, which Costard calls *selling a bargain well*" (Knight).

104. *Fast and loose.* A cheating game. See on i. 2. 155 above.

111. *And he ended the market.* Alluding to the proverb "Three women and a goose make a market" (Steevens).

115. *No feeling of it.* Costard plays on *sensibly*, which sometimes meant *feelingly* in the literal sense. Cf. *Cor.* i. 4. 53.

121. *Marry, Costard,* etc. The folio has "Sirra, Costard," etc. *Marry* is the conjecture of Knight and is favoured by the reply.

125. *Immured.* As in 2d folio, the earlier eds. having "emured."

130. *In lieu thereof.* In return for; the only meaning of the phrase in S. Cf. *Temp.* i. 2. 123, *M. of V.* iv. 1. 410, v. 1. 262, etc.

131. *Significant.* Armado's polysyllabic term for the letter.

133. *Ward.* Guard, preservation. For its use as a term in fencing (= posture of defence), cf. *Temp.* i. 2. 471 : "come from thy ward," etc.

135. *Like the sequel.* That is, like the sequel of a story. Some have fancied an allusion to the French *sequelle,* a gang of followers.

136. *Incony.* Apparently = fine, delicate. Nares cites examples of the word from Jonson, Marlowe, and others. It has been suggested that *Jew* is a colloquial contraction of *jewel.*

137. At this point lines 141-147 of iv. 1 probably belong. See note upon them there.

140. *Inkle.* Tape. Cf. *W. T.* iv. 1. 208, where *inkles* are mentioned among the wares of Autolycus.

153. *Good my knave.* My good boy. See on i. 2. 68 above. For *knave* = boy, servant, cf. *J. C.* iv. 3. 241, 269, *A. and C.* iv. 14. 12, etc.

172. *In print.* To the letter. Cf. *T. G. of V.* ii. 1. 175: "I will speak it in print," etc.

176. *Humorous.* Capricious. Cf. *K. John,* iii. 1. 119: "her humorous ladyship" (Fortune), etc.

177. *Critic.* Carper; the only sense in S. Cf. *Sonn.* 112. 10 and *T. and C.* v. 2. 131. See also on iv. 3. 168 below.

178. *Pedant.* Pedagogue; the only meaning in S. Cf. *T. N.* iii. 2. 80: "A pedant that keeps a school i' the church," etc.

179. *Magnificent!* Pompous, boastful; used by S. only here and in i. 1. 192 above.

180. *Wimpled.* Hoodwinked, blindfolded. Cf. Spenser, *F. Q.* i. 1. 4 : —

> " Yet she much whiter; but the same did hide
> Under a veil that wimpled was full low ; "

that is, drawn close about her face, like a *wimple*, a kind of veil.
Cf. *F. Q.* i. 12. 22 : —

> " For she had layd her mournefull stole aside,
> And widow-like sad wimple thrown away."

181. *Dan.* The folio has " don" (apparently the Spanish *Do*
= *dominus ;* as in *Much Ado*, v. 2. 86 : " Don Worm," etc.), which
might be retained; but *Dan* (the quarto " dan") is generally
adopted.

185. *Plackets.* Petticoats, or the slit or opening in those garments. *Placket-hole* is still used for the slit in a petticoat. The
codpiece was a part of the breeches in front, made very conspicuous
in the olden time.

187. *Paritors.* The same as *apparitors*, officers of ecclesiastical
courts whose duty it was to serve citations. Johnson says that they
are put under Cupid's government because the citations were most
frequently issued for offences against chastity.

188. *A corporal of his field.* Farmer says : " Giles Clayton, in
his *Martial Discipline*, 1591, has a chapter on the office and duty
of a *corporal of the field*." According to Tyrwhitt, his duties were
similar to those of an aide-de-camp now.

189. *Like a tumbler's hoop.* Alluding to its being adorned with
coloured ribbons.

191. *A German clock.* Clocks were then chiefly imported from
Germany, and the dramatists of the time were fond of comparing
the feminine " make-up " to their intricate machinery. Steevens
cites, among other passages, *Westward Hoe*, 1607 : " no German
clock, no mathematical engine whatsoever, requires so much repa-
ration ; " and *A Mad World, my Masters*, 1608 : —

> " She consists of a hundred pieces,
> Much like your German clock, and near allied :
> Both are so nice they cannot go for pride."

192. *Out of frame.* Out of order; as in *Ham.* i. 2. 20: "disjoint and out of frame."

197. *Wightly.* The early eds. have "whitly" or "whitely," which some explain as = whitish, pale (Dyce makes it = sallow); but Rosaline was dark. It seems probable that the word was a misspelling of *wightly,* which the Cambridge editors substitute, and which means nimble, sprightly. Spenser has both *wightly* and *wight* in this sense, and the latter is found in Chaucer; as in *C. T.* 14273 (Tyrwhitt's ed.): "With any yong man, were he never so wight," etc.

198. *Pitch-balls.* Black eyes were not esteemed beautiful in the time of S. Cf. *A. Y. L.* iii. 5. 47, where Rosalind refers contemptuously to Phebe's "bugle eyeballs," which the shepherdess afterwards recalls: "He said mine eyes were black." See also *Sonn.* 127.

199. *Do the deed.* Cf. *M. of V.* i. 3. 86: "And in the doing of the deed of kind," etc.

200. *Argus.* For other allusions to the hundred-eyed guardian of Io, see *M. of V.* v. 1. 230 and *T. and C.* i. 2. 31.

206. *Joan.* Often = a peasant, or a woman in humble life. Cf. v. 2. 918 below. See also *K. John,* i. 1. 184: "now can I make any Joan a lady."

ACT IV

Scene I.—1. *Was that the king,* etc. "This is just one of those touches that S. throws in, to mark the way in which a woman unconsciously betrays her growing preference for a man who loves her. The princess recognizes the horseman, though he is at such a distance that her attendant lord is unable to distinguish whether it be the king or not; and then she immediately covers her self-betrayal by the pretendedly indifferent words, *Whoe'er he was,* etc. S. in no one of his wondrous and numerous instances of insight into the human heart more marvellously manifests his magic power of

perception than in his discernment of the workings of female
nature; its delicacies, its subtleties, its reticences, its revelations,
its innocent reserves, and its artless confessions. He, of all masculine writers, was most truly feminine in his knowledge of what
passes within a woman's heart, and the multiform ways in which it
expresses itself through a woman's acts, words, manner — nay even
her very silence. He knew the eloquence of a look, the signifi-
cance of a gesture, the interpretation of a tacit admission; and,
moreover, he knew how to convey them in his might of expression
by ingenious inference" (Clarke).

10. *Stand.* Used in the technical sense of the hunter's station
or hiding-place when waiting for game. Cf. *Cymb.* ii. 3. 75, iii. 4.
111, *M. W.* v. 5. 248, etc. Knight remarks: "Royal and noble
ladies, in the days of Elizabeth, delighted in the somewhat unre-
fined sport of shooting deer with a cross-bow. In the 'alleys green'
of Windsor or of Greenwich parks, the queen would take her stand,
on an elevated platform, and, as the pricket or the buck was driven
past her, would aim the death-shaft, amid the acclamations of her
admiring courtiers. The ladies, it appears, were skilful enough at
this sylvan butchering. Sir Francis Leake writes to the Earl of
Shrewsbury — 'Your lordship has sent me a very great and fat stag,
the welcomer being stricken by your right honourable lady's hand.'
The practice was as old as the romances of the Middle Ages. But,
in those days, the ladies were sometimes not so expert as the Count-
ess of Shrewsbury; for, in the history of Prince Arthur, a fair hunt-
ress wounds Sir Launcelot of the Lake, instead of the stag at which
she aims."

17. *Fair.* For its use as a noun, cf. *M. N. D.* i. 1. 182, *A. Y. L.*
iii. 2. 99, etc. See also 22 just below.

18. *Good my glass.* My good glass; referring sportively to the
forester. Johnson supposed the *glass* to be "a small mirror set in
gold hanging at her girdle," according to the fashion of French
ladies at that time — and of English ladies also, as Stubbes tells us
in his *Anatomie of Abuses:* "they must haue their looking glasses

caryed with them whersoeuer they go. And good reason, for els how cold they see the deuil in them?"

23. *Foul.* Plain; opposed to *fair*, as often.

25. *Accounted ill.* Because not consistent with *mercy*, as missing the mark would rather be.

35. *That my heart means no ill.* That is, means no ill *to*. *That* is treated like the dative *him* in "never meant him any ill" (2 *Hen. VI.* ii. 3. 91), etc.

36. *Curst.* Shrewish; as often.

Self-sovereignty. "Not a sovereignty *over*, but *in* themselves. So *self-sufficiency, self-consequence*," etc. (Malone). Schmidt takes it to be = "that self sovereignty," or that same sovereignty, which is better.

37. *Praise sake.* The possessive inflection is often omitted before *sake* when the noun ends in a sibilant, and sometimes in other cases. Cf. "fashion sake" (*A. Y. L.* iii. 2. 271), "oath sake" (*T. N.* iii. 4. 326), etc.

41. *The commonwealth.* That is, of the "new-modelled society" of the king and his associates (Mason). Johnson makes it = "the common people."

42. *God dig-you-den.* God give you good even. Cf. *R. and J.* i. 2. 57, ii. 4. 116, *Cor.* ii. 1. 193, iv. 6. 20, etc.

56. *Break up this capon.* That is, open this letter. Here *break up* is = the preceding *carve*. It is applied to opening a despatch (the "sealed-up oracle") in *W. T.* iii. 2. 132: "Break up the seals and read." See also *M. of V.* ii. 4. 10: "to break up this" (a letter). *Capon* is used like *poulet* in French for a love-letter. Farmer quotes Henry IV. as saying: "My niece of Guise would please me best, notwithstanding the malicious reports that she loves *poulets* in paper better than in a fricasee." Note the rhyme of *serve* (pronounced *sarve*) with *carve ;* and cf. the rhymes of *convert* and *desert* with *part, art*, etc., in *Sonn.* 11. 4, 14. 12, 17. 2, 49. 10, and 72. 6. On the other hand, *kerve* is an old spelling of *carve*, and it may have been so pronounced in the time of S.

57. *Importeth.* Concerneth.

58. *Swear.* The rhyme with *here* suggests that it may have been pronounced *sweer* (Furness); or *ea* and *e* in both = *ā*.

65. *Illustrate.* Illustrious; used again by Holofernes in v. 1. 122 below. It is often used by Chapman; as in *Iliad,* xi.: "Illustrate Hector." For *King Cophetua,* see on i. 2. 110 above.

68. *Annothanize.* Explain. The quartos and 1st folio have "annothanize," the later folios "anatomize," which many eds. follow. Either word would suit Armado well enough.

87–92. *Thus dost thou hear,* etc. These lines are appended to the letter as a quotation, and Warburton thought that they were really from some ridiculous poem of the time. The *Nemean lion* is mentioned again in *Ham.* i. 4. 83, where *Nemean* is accented as here on the first syllable.

92. *Repasture.* Repast, food; used by S. only here.

96. *Going o'er it.* For the play upon *style,* see on i. 1. 200 above. *Erewhile* = just now.

98. *Phantasime.* Fantastic; as in v. 1. 18 below, but nowhere else in S. *Monarcho* was the name of an Italian, a fantastic character of the time, referred to by Meres, Nash, Churchyard, and other writers. See p. 17 above.

107. *Suitor?* This seems to have been pronounced *shooter,* and that is the spelling of the early eds. here. Steevens and Malone quote sundry passages from contemporary writers illustrating the old pronunciation. In *A. and C.* v. 2. 105, Pope and Malone took the "suites" or "suits" of the folio to be an error for "shoots." Here, however, Furness thinks that "shooter" (in the literal sense) should be retained; and this, as he says, is favoured by Rosaline's reply, "Why, *she* that bears the bow."

108. *My continent of beauty.* That is, embodiment of beauty. Cf. *Ham.* v. 2. 115: "you shall find in him the continent of what part a gentleman would see." S. uses the word only in this etymological sense of *container.*

113. *Your deer.* The play on *deer* and *dear* was a favourite

one. Cf. *V. and A.* 231, *P. P.* 300, *M. W.* v. 5. 18, 123, *T. of S.* v. 2. 56, 1 *Hen. IV.* v. 4. 107, *Macb.* iv. 3. 206, etc.

114. *By the horns.* The much-worn joke on the horns of the cuckold.

122. *Queen Guinever.* The unfaithful queen of Arthur; mentioned by S. only here.

131. *Prick.* The point in the centre of the *mark*, or target. *Mete at* = to measure with the eye in aiming, hence to aim at.

132. *Wide o' the bow-hand.* "A good deal to the left of the mark; a term still retained in modern archery" (Douce). The *bow-hand* was the hand holding the bow, or the left hand.

133. *Clout.* "The white mark at which archers took their aim. The *pin* was the wooden pin that upheld it" (Steevens). Cf. 2 *Hen. IV.* iii. 2. 51 and *Lear*, iv. 6. 92; and for *pin*, *R. and J.* ii. 4. 15.

136. *Greasily.* Grossly; the only instance of the word in S.

138. *Rubbing.* A term in bowling. Cf. *T. and C.* iii. 2. 52. The noun *rub* in the same sense occurs often figuratively; as in *K. John,* iii. 4. 128, *Hen. V.* ii. 2. 188, v. 2. 33, etc.

141–147. *O' my troth . . . nit !* These lines are evidently out of place, and Staunton was probably right in supposing that they belong after line 136 ("My sweet ounce," etc.) in iii. 1, where I put them in my former edition. It now seems to me better to leave them where they stand in the early eds., as Staunton did, though I still believe that they belong elsewhere. There is no line rhyming to 141, and some suppose one to have been lost; but it is quite as probable that 141 is either an interpolation, or a line struck out by the poet in revising the play, but accidentally retained by the transcriber or printer. See on iv. 3. 298 below.

143. *Armado o' th' one side.* The 1st quarto has "Armatho ath toothen side," and the folio "*Armathor* ath to the side." The text is due to Rowe.

147. *Pathetical.* The word has already been used by Armado in i. 2. 92 above. Just what either he or Costard means by it must

be matter of conjecture. S. has it nowhere else, except in *A. Y. L.*
iv. 1. 196, where it appears to be also an affectation. For the personal use of *nit*, cf. *T. of S.* iv. 3. 110, the only other instance of
the word in S.

148. *Sola, sola!* Costard hears the noise of the hunters, and
runs to join them, with a shout to attract their attention. Cf.
M. of V. v. 1. 39, where Launcelot enters with the same cry.

SCENE II. — 3. *Sanguis, in blood. In blood* was a term of the
chase = in full vigour. Cf. 1 *Hen. VI.* iv. 2. 48: "If we be English
deer, be then in blood," etc. Some regard *sanguis* as a blunder
for the Italian *sanguigno* (full of blood), and *cœlo* as for *cielo*
(Italian).

4. *Pomewater.* A kind of apple. Steevens quotes an old ballad:
"Whose cheeks did resemble two rosting pomewaters." In *The
Puritan*, "the pomewater of his eye" is = the apple of his eye.

10. *A buck of the first head.* According to *The Return from
Parnassus*, 1606 (quoted by Steevens), "a buck is the first year, a
fawn; the second year, a *pricket;* the third year, a sorrell; the
fourth year, a soare; the fifth, a *buck of the first head;* the sixth
year, a compleat buck."

11. *Sir.* The title *Sir* was formerly applied to priests and
curates in general. Nares explains the usage thus: "*Dominus*,
the academical title of a bachelor of arts, was usually rendered by
Sir in English at the universities; therefore, as most clerical persons had taken that first degree, it became usual to style them *Sir*."
Latimer speaks of "a Sir John, who hath better skill in playing at
tables, or in keeping a garden, then in God's word."

18. *Unconfirmed.* Inexperienced, ignorant; as in *Much Ado*,
iii. 3. 124: "That shows thou art unconfirmed."

22. *Twice-sod. Sod*, like *sodden*, is the participle of *seethe*. Cf.
R. of L. 1592: "sod in tears," etc. *Twice-sod simplicity* = con-
centrated stupidity, as if boiled down.

29. *Which we*, etc. In the folio this reads: "which we taste

and feeling, are for those parts," etc. Various emendations have been proposed, of which Tyrwhitt's in the text seems the best, and is adopted by the majority of recent editors.

31. *Patch.* A play on the word in its sense of fool, for which see *M. of V.* ii. 5. 46, or *M. N. D.* iii. 2. 9. Johnson says: "The meaning is, to be in a school would as ill become a *patch* as folly would become me."

36. *Dictynna.* One of the names of Diana. Steevens suggests that S. may have found the word in Golding's *Ovid:* "Dictynna garded with her traine, and proud of killing deere ; " but he had probably read the original Latin (*Met.* ii. 441) in school.

40. *Raught.* An old past tense and participle of *reach.* For its use as the former, cf. *Hen. V.* iv. 6. 21; and as the latter, *A. and C.* iv. 9. 30.

41. *The allusion holds in the exchange.* "The riddle is as good when I use the name of Adam as when I use the name of Cain" (Warburton). Mr. Brae takes *allusion* to be used in the strict Latin sense of "play, joke, or jest," and makes *exchange* = "the changing of the moon."

55. *Affect the letter.* "Practise alliteration" (Mason). For another satire on this affectation of the time, cf. *M. N. D.* v. 1. 145 fol.

58. *Some say a sore.* For *sore*, or *soare*, as applied to a deer "of the fourth year," see on 10 above; also for *sorel* in the next line.

61. *O sore L !* The 1st quarto has "o sorell," and the folios "O sorell." The reading in the text is Capell's, and is generally adopted. The Cambridge ed. has "makes fifty sores one sorel," which is plausible and perhaps favoured by the next line.

64. *If a talent be a claw.* The play on *talent* and *talon* is obvious. The latter word was sometimes written *talent.* Malone cites, among other instances, Marlowe's *Tamburlaine*, 1590 : —

> "and now doth ghastly death
> With greedy tallents gripe my bleeding heart."

Claw was sometimes = humour, flatter. Cf. *Much Ado*, i. 3. 18: "claw no man in his humour." The origin of the metaphor is illustrated by 2 *Hen. IV*. ii. 4. 282. Reed quotes Wilson, *Discourse upon Usury*, 1572: "therefore I will clawe him, and saye well might he fare, and godds blessing have he too. For the more he speaketh, the better it itcheth, and maketh better for me."

69. *Ventricle of memory*. The brain was supposed to have three ventricles or chambers, one of which was the seat of memory.

70. *Pia mater*. The membrane covering the brain, used for the brain itself; as in *T. N.* i. 5. 123 and *T. and C.* ii. 1. 77. *Upon the mellowing of occasion* = at "the very riping of the time" (*M. of V.* ii. 8. 40), or when the fit occasion comes. See also *T. N.* i. 2. 43: "Till I had made my own occasion mellow;" that is, till the time was ripe. So *mellowed* = ripe in *Rich. III.* iii. 7. 168, etc.

83. *Person*. "Parson" (the reading of the 2d folio). Steevens quotes Holinshed: "Jerom was vicar of Stepnie, and Garrard was person of Honielane," etc. Staunton adds from Selden, *Table Talk:* "Though we write *Parson* differently, yet 't is but *Person;* that is, the individual Person set apart for the service of the Church, and 't is in Latin *Persona*, and *Personatus* is a *Personage*." For the play on *pierce* (which was perhaps pronounced *perse*), cf. 1 *Hen. IV*. v. 3. 59. *Pierce* rhymes with *rehearse* in *Rich. II.* v. 3. 127.

97. *Mantuan!* Giovanni Battista Spagnuoli (or Spagnoli), named *Mantuanus* from his birthplace, who died in 1516, was the author of certain *Eclogues* which the pedants of that day preferred to Virgil's, and which were read in schools. The 1st Eclogue begins with the passage quoted by Holofernes. Malone quotes references to Mantuanus from Nash and Drayton. A translation of his Latin poems by George Turbervile was printed in 1567. Mr. Andrew Lang, in his comments on this play (*Harper's Magazine*, May, 1893), takes the Mantuan to be Virgil, as other critics have sometimes done.

99. *Venetia*, etc. In the folio this reads: "*vemchie, vencha, que non te vnde, que non te perreche,*" which exactly follows the 1st quarto. The text is taken by the Cambridge editors from Florio's *Second Frutes*, 1591, whence the poet probably got it. There it has the second line, "Ma chi te vede, ben gli costa." In Howell's *Letters,* it appears with a translation, thus: —

> "Venetia, Venetia, chi non te vede, non te pregia,
> Ma chi t' ha troppo veduto te dispregia.
>
> Venice, Venice, none thee unseen can prize;
> Who thee hath seen too much, will thee despise."

It is usually printed in the form in which Theobald gives it: —

> "Vinegia, Vinegia,
> Chi non te vede, ei non te pregia."

108. *If love*, etc. This sonnet appears, with a few verbal variations, in *P. P.* v.

112. *Bias.* Originally a term in bowling. Cf. *T. of S.* iv. 5. 25, *Rich. II.* iii. 4. 5, etc.

118. *Thy voice*, etc. Malone compares *A. and C.* v. 2. 83: —

> "his voice was propertied
> As all the tuned spheres, and that to friends;
> But when he meant to quail and shake the orb
> He was as rattling thunder."

122. *You find not the apostrophas.* Knight understands this to refer to the apostrophes in *vow'd* and *bow'd* (109 and 111 above) and therefore prints these "vowed" and "bowed." It more probably refers to the metrical imperfection in the last line of the poem, which should be an Alexandrine. In the 1st quarto *sings* is printed *singes,* which may have been intended as a dissyllable. Some editors read "sings the," and others "singeth." The *New Eng. Dict.* suggests that *apostrophas* should be "apostrophus" (the mark of omission), and Furness believes that it certainly should.

128. *Imitari.* To imitate (Latin).

129. *The tired horse.* The early eds. have "tyred" for *tired*

(= attired, or arrayed). It is possibly another allusion to Bankes's horse (see on i. 2. 52 above), as Farmer explains it ; *tired* being = "adorned with ribbons." *Tired* may, however, have its ordinary meaning ; the horse sympathizing with his master, as in *Sonn.* 50. 5 :

> " The beast that bears me, tired with my woe,
>   Plods dully on," etc.

132. *Ay, sir, from one Monsieur Biron.* "S. forgot himself in this passage. Jaquenetta knew nothing of Biron, and had said just before that the letter had been sent to her from Don Armado and given to her by Costard" (Mason). There is probably some corruption, but no satisfactory emendation has been suggested.

136. *Intellect.* Used peculiarly for "sense, purport" (*New Eng. Dict.*) and explained by what follows. Baynes may, however, be right in making it = signature.

145. *Stay not thy compliment ; I forgive thy duty.* That is, do not tarry to make any formal obeisance ; I excuse you from that. Cf. *M. N. D.* iv. 1. 21 : "Pray you, leave your courtesy, good mounsieur."

154. *Colourable colours.* "That is, specious or fair-seeming appearances" (Johnson) ; or "false pretexts" (Schmidt). For *colour* (= pretext), cf. *M. W.* iv. 2. 168, *W. T.* iv. 4. 566, *J. C.* ii. 1. 29, etc.

158. *Before repast.* The quarto reading. The folio has " (being repast)," which might mean "being repasted," or having dined.

161. *Ben venuto.* Welcome (Italian). It is used again in *T. of S.* i. 2. 282.

167. *Certes.* Certainly. Cf. *Temp.* iii. 3. 30, *C. of E.* iv. 4. 78, etc. Schmidt considers it monosyllabic in *Hen. VIII.* i. 1. 48 and *Oth.* i. 1. 16.

169. *Pauca verba.* Few words (Latin).

SCENE III. — **2.** *Pitched a toil.* Set a net. *Toiling in a pitch* alludes to Rosaline's complexion (Johnson) ; or her black eyes (Furness). Cf. iii. 1. 198 above.

4. *Set thee down, Sorrow!* A proverbial expression. Cf. i. 1. 296 above.

5. *And ay the fool.* The folio has "I" for *ay*, as regularly, and the editors generally take it for the personal pronoun. They may be right, but *ay* (= ever) gives essentially the same meaning : "and so say I, and ever the fool in doing it." White makes *ay* a verb = "confirm."

7. *It kills sheep.* Alluding to the story that Ajax, when the arms of Hector were adjudged to Ulysses instead of himself, slew a whole flock of sheep, which, in his insane fury, he mistook for the sons of Atreus. In *ay, a sheep*, the *ay* is used, as often, for emphasis : "it kills me, verily a sheep."

12. *Lie in my throat.* A common expression. Cf. *T. N.* iii. 4. 172, *Rich. III.* i. 2. 93, etc.

18. *If the other three were in.* That is, in the same predicament with himself.

20. *Gets up into a tree.* The old stage-direction is "*He stands aside ;*" which was all that the humble scenic arrangements of that day could afford ; but it is evident from 77 below that Biron is meant to be above the others.

23. *Bird-bolt.* A blunt-headed arrow, used to kill birds without piercing them. Cf. *Much Ado*, i. 1. 42 and *T. N.* i. 5. 100.

28. *The night of dew.* The dewy night, the tears of sorrow. The lady's *eye-beams* are the morning sunshine on these dew-drops of his grief. Cf. *V. and A.* 481 fol.

31. *As doth thy face*, etc. Malone compares *V. and A.* 491 : —

> "But hers, which through the crystal tears gave light,
> Shone like the moon in water seen by night."

34. *Triumphing.* Accented on the second syllable ; as in *R. of L.* 1388, 1 *Hen. IV.* v. 3. 15, v. 4. 14, *Rich. III.* iii. 4. 91, iv. 4. 59, etc.

46. *Perjure.* Perjurer. "The punishment of perjury is to wear on the breast a paper expressing the crime" (Johnson). Steevens quotes several references to the penalty.

51. *Corner-cap.* The *biretta*, or three-cornered cap of the Catholic priest. Marshall quotes *The New Custom*, 1573: "he will have priests no corner-cap to wear."

53. *Love's Tyburn.* The gallows at Tyburn was sometimes of triangular form.

57. *Guards.* Facings, trimmings. Cf. *Much Ado*, i. 1. 289: "the guards are but slightly basted on," etc. For *hose* = breeches, see *A. Y. L.* ii. 7. 160, etc.

58. *Slop.* *Slops* were large loose trowsers. Cf. *2 Hen. IV.* i. 2. 34: "my short cloak and my slops;" *R. and J.* ii. 4. 47: "your French slop." Steevens quotes Jonson, *Alchemist:*—

> "six great slops
> Bigger than three Dutch hoys."

Did not the heavenly rhetoric, etc. This sonnet also appears in *P. P.* iii. A comparison of the two versions will show some slight verbal differences.

71. *To lose an oath.* By losing an oath. This "indefinite use" of the infinitive is very common in S.

72. *The liver-vein.* For the liver as the seat of love, cf. *Temp.* iv. 1. 56: "the ardour of my liver;" *Much Ado*, iv. 1. 253: "If ever love had interest in his liver," etc.

76. *All hid, all hid.* "The children's cry at *hide and seek*" (Musgrave).

79. *More sacks to the mill!* The name of a boyish sport.

80. *Woodcocks.* The bird was supposed to have no brains, and hence was a common metaphor for a fool. Cf. *T. of S.* i. 2. 161, *A. W.* iv. 1. 100, etc.

84. *She is not, corporal.* Biron styles Dumain *corporal* as he has before called himself "a *corporal* of his (Love's) field," with perhaps an allusion to the word *mortal* just used by Dumain.

85. *Quoted.* Noted, marked. Cf. *K. John*, iv. 2. 222:—

> "A fellow by the hand of nature mark'd,
> Quoted and sign'd to do a deed of shame," etc.

See also v. 2. 784 below.   In the early eds. the word is spelt "coted" in both passages, as it was pronounced.   The meaning is that "amber itself is regarded as foul when compared with her hair" (Mason).

87. *Stoop.*   Schmidt thinks this may be an adjective = crooked; and Herford so explains it.

94. *Reigns in my blood.*   For the figure, cf. *Ham.* iv. 3. 68: "For like the hectic in my blood he rages."

95. *Incision.*   Blood-letting; the only sense in S.   Cf. *M. of V.* ii. 1. 6, *A. Y. L.* iii. 2. 75, *Rich. II.* i. 1. 155, *Hen. V.* iv. 2. 9, etc.

96. *Misprision!*   Mistake, misapprehension.   Cf. *Much Ado*, iv. 1. 187: "some strange misprision."

97. *Saucers.*   Bleeding in fevers was common in the time of S.; and the barber-surgeons used to exhibit saucers of blood as the sign of their profession (Halliwell-Phillipps).

99. *On a day*, etc.   This poem is in *P. P.* xvii., and also in *England's Helicon*, 1614.

104. *Can passage find.*   In the *P. P.* we find "gan" for *can*. The latter is an old spelling of *gan*.   Cf. Spenser, *F. Q.* i. 4. 46: "With gentle words he can her fayrely greet," etc.

105. *That.*   So that; as in v. 2. 9 below.

106. *Wish'd.*   The reading in *P. P.* and the 2d folio; the quartos and 1st folio have "wish."

109. *Is sworn.*   "Hath sworn" in *P. P.* and *England's Helicon*.

110. *Thorn.*   "Throne" in the early eds. and *P. P.;* corrected by Rowe from *England's Helicon*.

133 *Wreathed.*   Folded.   Cf. *T. G. of V.* ii. 1. 19: "to wreathe your arms," etc.

148. *Know so much by me.*   That is, about me.   Cf. *A. W.* v. 3. 237: "By him and by this woman here what know you ?"   See also 1 *Corinthians*, iv. 4: "I know nothing by myself" (that is, against myself).

149. *Advancing.*   White has "*Descends*," and remarks: "The original has no stage-direction here.   It is noteworthy that Biron

does not say 'Now I *descend*,' but 'Now *step I forth*,' which betrays
the poet's consciousness that, although he imagined the character
to be in a tree, the actor who played it would be on the same plane
with the others." I am inclined, however, to think that "*Advancing*" is the proper stage-direction, and that *step I forth* refers to his
coming forward *after* descending from the tree.

153. *Coaches; in*, etc. The early eds. have "couches in," etc.;
corrected by Hanmer. Cf. 30 above.

156. *Like of*. See on i. 1. 107 above.

159. *Mote . . . mote*. The early eds. have "moth." Cf. p. 154
above.

162. *Teen*. Grief, pain. Cf. *Temp.* i. 2. 64: "To think o' the
teen that I have turn'd you to," etc.

164. *Gnat!* That is, an insignificant creature. Schmidt compares *Per.* ii. 3. 62: "And princes not doing so are like to gnats."
Mason says: "Biron is abusing the king for his sonneting like a
minstrel, and compares him to a *gnat*, which always sings as it
flies." From the context it is quite as likely that *gnat* is simply
a hit at the king for "coming down" to such petty business as
love-making.

165. *Gig*. A kind of top. Cf. v. 1. 67, 69 below. S. uses the
word nowhere else.

166. *Profound*. Accented on the first syllable because coming
before a noun accented on the first syllable. Cf. *Ham.* iv. 1. 1:
"There's matter in these sighs, these profound heaves." See, on
the other hand, v. 2. 52 below, or *Sonn.* 112. 9. See also on i. 1.
136 above.

167. *Push-pin*. A child's game.

168. *Critic Timon*. Cynical Timon. See on iii. 1. 177 above.
S. uses the adjective only here, but we have *critical* = censorious,
in *M. N. D.* v. 1. 54 and *Oth.* ii. 1. 120 (the only instances of the
word).

172. *A caudle, ho!* A *caudle* was a warm, cordial drink, often
used for the sick. The folios misprint "candle" (the 1st quarto

has *caudle*), as in 2 *Hen. VI.* iv. 7. 95, the only other instance of
the noun in S.

178. *With men*, etc. The folio has "with men, like men of
inconstancie" ("strange inconstancy" in later folios). The text
was suggested by Walker, and is adopted by Dyce, the Cambridge
editors, and others.

181. *Pruning me*. Adorning myself. "The metaphor is taken
from a cock, who in his pride *prunes himself;* that is, picks off the
loose feathers, to smooth the rest. To *prune* and to *plume*, spoken
of a bird, is the same" (Johnson). Cf. *Cymb.* v. 4. 118 :—

> " his royal bird
> Prunes the immortal wing," etc.

183. *State*. Mode of *standing*, as opposed to *gait;* attitude.
Cf. *station* in *Ham.* iii. 4. 58 and *A. and C.* iii. 3. 22.

185. *True man*. Often opposed to *thief*. Cf. *Much Ado*, iii.
3. 54, etc.

187. *Present*. Document to be *presented*. Some see an allusion
to the legal formula "Be it known to all men by these presents ;"
but this seems unnecessary.

188. *Makes*. Does. Cf. *A. Y. L.* i. 1. 31 : "What make you
here?" This use of the word was very common, and is played
upon, as here, in *Rich. III.* i. 3. 164 fol.

192. *Person*. Parson ; the reading of the early eds. See on
iv. 2. 83 above.

199. *Toy*. Trifle ; as in 168 above. Cf. 1 *Hen. VI.* iv. 1. 145:
"a toy, a thing of no regard," etc.

205. *Mess*. Sometimes = a party of *four*, as "at great dinners
the company was usually arranged into fours" (Nares). Cf. v. 2.
363 below, and see also 3 *Hen. VI.* i. 4. 73: "your mess of
sons."

210. *Turtles*. Turtle-doves ; the only sense in S. Cf. v. 2. 903
below.

Sirs. The plural is mostly used in addressing persons of lower rank than the speaker, and sometimes women are included, as here. Cf. *A. and C.* iv. 15. 85, and *Sirrah* in *Id.* v. 2. 229.

217. *Of all hands.* "At any rate, in any case" (Schmidt). Some make it = "on all sides, on every account."

221. *Gorgeous east.* Milton has adopted this in *P. L.* ii. 3: "Or where the gorgeous east with richest hand," etc.

222. *Strucken.* The early eds. have "strooken." Other old forms are *stroken, strook,* and *stricken.*

238. *To things of sale,* etc. Malone quotes *Sonn.* 21. 14: "I will not praise that purpose not to sell."

251. *No face,* etc. Cf. *Sonn.* 132. 13: —

> "Then will I swear beauty herself is black,
> And all they foul that thy complexion lack."

See also *Sonn.* 127.

253. *Shade.* The early eds. have "schoole" or "school." Various changes have been suggested; as "scowl," "stole," "soul," "soil," "scroll," "shroud," "seal," and "suit."

254. *And beauty's crest,* etc. "*Crest* is here properly opposed to *badge. Black,* says the king, is the *badge of hell,* but that which graces the heaven is the *crest of beauty. Black* darkens hell, and is therefore hateful; *white* adorns heaven, and is therefore lovely" (Johnson). Tollet says: "In heraldry, a *crest* is a device placed above a coat of arms. S. therefore uses it in a sense equivalent to *top* or *utmost height.*" Cf. *K. John,* iv. 3. 46.

257. *Usurping hair.* On Shakespeare's repugnance to false hair, cf. *M. of V.* iii. 2. 92, *T. of A.* iv. 3. 144, *Sonn.* 68. 5, etc. For his allusions to *painting,* cf. *M. for M.* iii. 2. 83, iv. 2. 40, *T. of A.* iv. 3. 147, *Ham.* v. 1. 213, *W. T.* iv. 4, 101, etc.

266. *Crack.* Boast. Cf. *Cymb.* v. 5. 177: —

> "our brags
> Were crack'd of kitchen-trulls."

276. *Here's thy love.* Alluding of course to his black shoe.

Johnson thought it necessary to insert an explanatory stage-direction, and many editors follow him.

284. *Flattery.* "Gratifying deception" (Schmidt), or "soothing remedy" (Herford).

286. *Quillets.* Casuistries, subtleties, nice distinctions of logic or law. Cf. 1 *Hen. VI.* ii. 4. 17: "these nice sharp quillets of the law;" *Ham.* v. 1. 108: "his quiddits now, his quillets," etc.

295. *Book.* Some editors put a colon or semicolon after this word.

297–302. *For when . . . fire.* These lines are evidently a part of the first sketch of the play accidentally retained in the revision. They are repeated in new form below. The same is true of 310–317 below. See p. 11 above.

303. *Poisons up.* For the intensive use of *up*, cf. "kill them up" in *A. Y. L.* ii. 1. 62. See also *flatter up* in v. 2. 812 below. Many editors follow Theobald in reading "prisons up;" but the simile which follows seems to favour the old text. There is a closer analogy between *poisoning* and *tiring* than between *prisoning* and *tiring*. The early eds. all have "poysons." The Cambridge editors, after adopting "prisons," return to *poisons* in the Globe ed.

311. *Teaches such beauty,* etc. "That is, a lady's eyes give a fuller notion of *beauty* than any author" (Johnson).

317. *Our books.* "That is, our *true* books, from which we derive most information — the *eyes* of women" (Malone).

320. *Numbers.* "Poetical measures" (Johnson).

322. *Keep.* Occupy, hold.

334. *When the suspicious head of theft is stopp'd.* "That is, a lover in pursuit of his mistress has his sense of hearing quicker than a *thief* (who suspects every sound he hears) in pursuit of his prey" (Warburton).

335. *Sensible.* Sensitive; as in *Temp.* ii. 1. 174: "sensible and nimble lungs," etc.

338. *Valour.* The reference is of course to the daring of Her-

cules in attempting to get the golden apples. *Hesperides* is used for the Gardens of the Hesperides. Cf. *Per.* i. 1. 27 : —

> " Before thee stands this fair Hesperides,
> With golden fruit, but dangerous to be touch'd ;
> For death-like dragons here affright thee hard."

Malone quotes Greene's *Friar Bacon*, etc., 1598 : "That watch'd the garden call'd Hesperides."

342. *Voice.* Possibly the word is a plural, like *sense* in *Sonn.* 112. 10, etc. The plural verb may, however, be explained as an instance of "confusion of proximity." The meaning of the passage may be, "When love speaks, the accordant voice of all the gods makes heaven drowsy with the harmony" (Clarke) ; or, perhaps, when love speaks, it is *like* the voices of all the gods blended in soul-soothing harmony.

356. *A word that loves all men.* Malone thinks this means "that is pleasing to all men," and compares the *impersonal* use of "it likes me" = it pleases me. Of course there is no analogy whatever between the two. The expression was used for the sake of the antithesis, and probably with a somewhat loose reference to the idea that love affects all men, or, possibly, is a blessing to all men. Herford suggests : " probably the contrast intended is between wisdom, which all profess to admire, and love, which attracts them by an irresistible magnetism, whether they will or no."

367. *Get the sun of them.* As Malone notes, it was an advantage in the days of archery to have the sun at the back of the bowmen and in the face of the enemy ; as Henry V. found at the battle of Agincourt. There is a play on *sun* and *son.*

368. *Glozes.* Sophistries, special pleadings ; the only instance of the noun in S. For the verb, see *Hen. V.* i. 2. 40, *T. and C.* ii. 2. 165, etc.

378. *Love.* Venus ; as often.

380. *Be time.* That is, be sufficient time (Clarke). Some read " betime " (= betide, chance), a verb which S. nowhere uses.

381. *Allons! allons!* Cf. v. 1. 152 below.

Sow'd cockle reap'd no corn. "This proverbial expression intimates that, beginning with perjury, they can expect to reap nothing but falsehood" (Warburton).

ACT V

Scene I. — 1. *Satis quod sufficit.* "Enough 's as good as a feast" (Steevens).

2. *Reasons.* Arguments; or, perhaps, as Johnson and others explain it, "discourse, conversation."

4. *Affection.* "Affectation" (2d folio). In *Ham.* ii. 2. 464, the quartos have "affection," the folios "affectation." See also on v. 2. 409 below. *Affectioned* (= affected) occurs in *T. N.* ii. 3. 160.

5. *Opinion.* Dogmatism; or, perhaps, self-conceit.

9. *Novi hominem tanquam te.* I know the man as well as I do you.

10. *His tongue filed.* His speech is polished or refined. Cf. *Sonn.* 85. 4: "And precious phrase by all the muses fil'd," etc.

12. *Thrasonical.* Boastful; like Thraso in Terence's *Eunuchus.* Cf. *A. Y. L.* v. 2. 34: "Cæsar's thrasonical brag," etc.

13. *Picked.* Over-refined, fastidious. Cf. *Ham.* v. 1. 151: "the age is grown so picked;" and *K. John,* i. 1. 193: "My picked man of countries." Travellers were much given to this affectation; which explains *peregrinate* here.

18. *Phantasimes.* Fantastics. See on iv. 1. 98 above. *Point-device* = finical, "up to the best mark devisable;" as in *A. Y. L.* iii. 2. 401: "you are rather point-device in your accoutrements." For *companions* used contemptuously (= fellows), cf. *J. C.* iv. 3. 138, *Cor.* v. 2. 65, *C. of E.* iv. 4. 64, etc.

19. *Rackers of orthography.* White remarks: "This passage has especial interest on account of its testimony to the condition of our language when it was written. In his pedagoguish wrath, the Pedant lets us know that consonants now silent were then heard

on the lips of purists, that compound words preserved the forms and sounds of their elements, and that vowels were pronounced more purely and openly than they now are. The change from the ancient to what may be called the modern pronunciation appears to have begun, among the more cultivated classes, just before S. commenced his career, and to have been completed in the course of about fifty years — that is, from about 1575 to about 1625. . . . With regard to the completion of this change, the following passages from Charles Butler's *English Grammar*, Oxford, 1633, are decisive: 'Another use of the letters is to show the derivation of a word: namely, when we keep a letter in the derivative, &c. . . . also when a letter not sounded in the English is yet written, because it is in the language from which the word came: as *b* in *debt, doubt; e* in *George; g* in *deseign, flegme, reign, signe; h* in *Thomas, authoriti; l* in *salve*, &c. . . . *L* after *a* and before *f, v, k*, or *m* is vulgarly sounded like *u* (or, with the *a*, like the diphthong *au*); before *f* as in *calf, half;* before *v* as in *salv, calvs, halvs*, etc.'" It is doubtful, however, whether the *b* in *debt* and *doubt* was ever sounded; but *debit* was still in use in the sense of *debt*, and Holofernes may have pedantically assumed that both in *debt* and *doubt*, the *b* of the Latin original *ought* to be sounded.

24. *Abhominable.* The old spelling, and evidently also the pronunciation, of the word.

25. *Insinuateth me.* Intimates or suggests to me.

Ne intelligis? Do you understand? Johnson conjectures "nonne" for *ne*.

27. *Laus Deo*, etc. The folio reads here : —

" *Cura. Laus Deo, bene intelligo.*
Peda. Bome boon for boon prescian, a little scratcht, 'twil serue."

The reading in the text is due to Theobald, who says : "The curate, addressing with complaisance his brother pedant, says *bone* to him, as we frequently in Terence find *bone vir;* but the pedant, thinking he had mistaken the adverb, thus descants on it : ' *Bone — bone for bene:* Priscian a little scratched: 't will serve.' Alluding to the common phrase, *Diminuis Prisciani caput,* applied to such as speak false Latin." This is ingenious, but I doubt whether it is anything more than a plausible mending of a hopelessly corrupt passage. It is, however, much to be preferred to the modification of it in the modern editions that have adopted it. These, without exception (at least, so far as I am aware), read "bone intelligo," making Nathaniel actually wrong in the use of the adverb. It is hardly conceivable that he should be guilty of a blunder for which a schoolboy ought to be whipped ; and besides he has used the correct form in "omne bene," in iv. 2. 32 above — a fact which all the editors appear to have overlooked. It is certainly more reasonable to suppose, as Theobald does, that Nathaniel's *bone* is the vocative of the adjective, and that Holofernes takes it to be a slip for the adverb ; which is natural enough, as *bene intelligo* is a common phrase. Being a pedagogue, and used to hearing such blunders from his pupils, it does not occur to him that Nathaniel would not be likely to make them.

The Cambridge editors retain the *bene intelligo,* and make Holofernes reply : "Bon, bon, fort bon, Priscian ! a little scratched ; ′t will serve." They say : "Holofernes patronizingly calls Sir Nathaniel *Priscian,* but, pedagogue-like, will not admit his perfect accuracy." It seems improbable, however, that he would play the critic in a case like this, where the construction is so simple that no possible question could be raised about it. Besides, the pedant does not elsewhere quote French, and Latin might naturally be expected from him here.

30. *Videsne quis venit?* Do you see who is coming ?

31. *Video, et gaudeo.* I see, and rejoice.

38. *Alms-basket of words.* The refuse of words. As Malone notes, the refuse meat of families was put into a basket and given to the poor. He cites Florio's *Second Frutes,* 1591 : "Take away the table, fould up the cloth, and put all these pieces of broken meat into a basket for the poor."

41. *Honorificabilitudinitatibus.* "This word, whencesoever it comes, is often mentioned as the longest word known" (Johnson).

42. *Flap-dragon.* "Some small combustible body, fired at one end, and put afloat in a glass of liquor" (Johnson). Cf. *2 Hen. IV.* ii. 4. 267: "drinks off candle-ends for flap-dragons." Almonds, plums, or raisins were commonly used for the purpose.

46. *Horn-book.* The child's primer, the single page of which, set in a wooden frame, was covered with thin horn, to keep it from being soiled or torn. S. uses the word only here.

49. *Pueritia.* Literally, boyhood; used affectedly for *puer*, boy.

52. *Quis.* Who.

54. *The fifth, if I.* Knight says: "The pedant asks who is the silly sheep — quis, quis? 'The third of the five vowels if you repeat them,' says Moth; and the pedant does repeat them — a, e, I; the other two clinch it, says Moth, o, u (O you). This may appear a poor conundrum, and a low conceit, as Theobald has it, but the satire is in opposing the pedantry of the boy to the pedantry of the man, and making the pedant have the worst of it in what he calls 'a quick venew of wit.'"

59. *Venue.* Touch, hit; a fencing term. It is the same as *veney* in *M. W.* i. 1. 296.

60. *Home.* That is, a home thrust. Cf. v. 2. 634 below.

63. *Wit-old!* A play upon *wittol* (= cuckold), for which cf. *M. W.* ii. 2. 313; the only instance of the word in S. *Wittolly* (= cuckoldly) occurs in the same play, ii. 2. 283.

69. *Circum circa.* That is, round and round.

81. *Preambulate.* Come forward.

83. *Charge-house.* A word not found elsewhere, and possibly a corruption. Steevens thought it might be = "a free school" (apparently on the *lucus a non lucendo* principle), but it is more likely one at which a fee was charged. Capell takes it to be a corruption of *Charter-house*, as that word is of *Chartreuse*.

97. *Inward.* Confidential, private. Cf. *Rich. III.* iii. 4. 8:

"Who is most inward with the royal duke?" See also the noun in *M. for M.* iii. 2. 138.

98. *Remember thy courtesy.* This was a phrase of the time, bidding a person who had taken off his hat as an act of courtesy, to put it on again. Dr. Ingleby (*Shakes. Hermeneutics*, p. 74) is probably right in his explanation of the origin of the phrase: "It arose, we think, as follows: the *courtesy* was the temporary removal of the hat from the head, and that was finished as soon as the hat was replaced. If any one from ill-breeding or over-politeness stood uncovered for a longer time than was necessary to perform the simple act of courtesy, the person so saluted reminded him of the fact that the removal of the hat was a courtesy: and this was expressed by the euphemism 'Remember thy courtesy,' which thus implied 'Complete your courtesy, and replace your hat.'"

99. *Importunate.* The folio reading. The 1st quarto has "importunt," and the Cambridge ed. "important."

104. *Excrement.* The word is applied to the hair or beard in five out of six passages in which S. uses it. Cf. *C. of E.* ii. 2. 79, *M. of V.* iii. 2. 87, etc.

111. *Chuck.* A term of endearment. Cf. *Macb.* iii. 2. 45, *Oth.* iii. 4. 49, iv. 2. 24, etc.

112. *Antique.* The early eds. use *antique* and *antick* indiscriminately, but with the accent always on the first syllable. See also 132 below.

119. *The Nine Worthies.* Famous personages, often alluded to, and classed somewhat arbitrarily, like the Seven Wonders of the World. They were commonly said to be three Gentiles — Hector, Alexander, Julius Cæsar; three Jews — Joshua, David, Judas Maccabæus; and three Christians — Arthur, Charlemagne, Godfrey of Bouillon. In the present play we find Pompey and Hercules among the number. Cf. *2 Hen. IV.* ii. 4. 238: "ten times better than the Nine Worthies."

127. *Myself,* etc. There is some corruption here, and no satisfactory emendation has been suggested.

129. *Pass.* Pass as, represent. Some editors insert ' for " or " as."

135. *Present.* Represent; as in *Temp.* iv. 1. 167 : " When I presented Ceres," etc. See many instances of the word below.

140. *Make an offence gracious.* " Convert an offence against yourselves into a dramatic propriety " (Steevens).

147. *Fadge.* Suit, or turn out well ; as in *T. N.* ii. 2. 34 : " How will this fadge ? " S. uses the word only twice.

149. *Via !* Away (Italian) ; used as " an adverb of encouragement " (Florio).

152. *Allons !* Cf. iv. 3. 381 above.

154. *The hay.* A country-dance with winding or serpentine movements (*New Eng. Dict.*). To *dance the hay* was also used figuratively for performing sinuous movements or evolutions like those of the *hay.*

SCENE II. — 2. *Fairings.* Presents (originally, those bought at a fair) ; used by S. only here.

3. *A lady,* etc. Walker conjectures that this line and the next should be transposed ; but it is not an unnatural exclamation as it stands.

10. *Wax.* Grow ; with an obvious play on the noun.

12. *Shrewd.* Mischievous, evil ; the original sense of the word. Cf. *A. Y. L.* v. 4. 179 : " That have endur'd shrewd days and nights," etc. *Unhappy* seems to be = roguish ; as in *A. W.* iv. 5. 66 : " A shrewd knave and an unhappy." *Gallows* = one who deserves the gallows.

19. *Mouse.* Cf. *Ham.* iii. 4. 183 : " call you his mouse." See also *T. N.* i. 5. 69.

22. *Taking it in snuff.* A play on the sense of taking it ill, or being vexed at it. Cf. Hotspur's quibble in 1 *Hen IV.* i. 3. 41. See also *M. N. D.* v. 1. 254.

28. *Past cure is still past care.* For the proverb, cf. *Sonn.* 147. 9 : " Past cure I am, now reason is past care."

29. *Bandied.* Like *set* (= game), an allusion to tennis. Cf. *K. John,* v. 2. 107 and *Hen. V.* i. 2. 262. See also *R. and J.* ii. 5. 114.

33. *Favour.* Present; playing upon its sense of *face.* Cf. iv. 3. 257 above.

43. *Ware pencils.* Beware of pencils. *Ware* is not a contraction of *beware,* as generally printed. "Rosaline says that Biron had drawn her picture in his letter; and afterwards playing on the word *letter,* Katherine compares her to a text B. Rosaline in reply advises her to beware of pencils, that is, of drawing likenesses, lest she should retaliate; which she afterward does by comparing her to a red dominical letter, and calling her marks of the small-pox *O's*" (Mason). In the old calendars (as in some modern ones) the *dominical* letter denoting Sunday was printed in red. Marshall thinks that *pencils* is = *pensel,* or *pensil,* "a pennon fastened to the end of a lance;" and that the meaning is, "Be on your guard; she means fighting;" with perhaps a play on *pencil.*

46. *A pox of that jest!* Theobald considered this rather coarse in the mouth of a princess; but, as Farmer reminds him, only the small-pox is meant. Davison has a canzonet on his lady's "sicknesse of the poxe;" and Dr. Donne writes to his sister: "I found Pegge had the poxe — I humbly thank God, it hath not much disfigured her."

Beshrew was a mild form of imprecation; and *shrow* was another spelling of *shrew* (cf. *shew* and *show,* etc.), representing the pronunciation of the word. For the rhyme, cf. *T. of S.* iv. 1. 213, v. 2. 28, 188. Dyce omits *I,* as "in 29 out of 31 examples in S. *beshrew* is a mere exclamatory imprecation." The other instance of the verb with a pronoun expressed is in *R. and J.* v. 2. 26: "She will beshrew me much."

47. *But, Katherine,* etc. It has been conjectured that either *Katherine* should be omitted, or we should read "sent you from Dumain."

53. *Longaville.* Here rhyming with *mile*, as above (iv. 3. 132)
with *compile;* but in iv. 3. 122 with *ill.*

61. *In by the week !* A cant phrase of the time, sometimes = in
love, as in the old *Roister Doister* (Staunton).

65. *Hests.* The quartos and 1st folio have " device," and the
later folios "all to my behests." The reading in the text (cf. *Temp.*
i. 2. 274, iii. 1. 37, iv. 1. 65) was suggested by Walker; but perhaps that of the later folios is to be preferred.

66. *And make him proud,* etc. " Make him proud to flatter me
who make a mock of his flattery" (*Edin. Rev.* Nov. 1786).

67. *Potent-like.* The early eds. have " perttaunt-like " or " per-
taunt-like." Other emendations are " pedant-like," " portent-like,"
" pageant-like," " potently," and " persaunt-like " (= piercingly).
Potent-like is due to Singer. *Pertaunt* has not been satisfactorily
explained by the few who retain it.

69. *Catch'd.* For the form, cf. *A. W.* i. 3. 176 and *R. and J.* iv.
5. 48. We find it as the past tense in *Cor.* i. 3. 68.

78. *Simplicity.* Silliness; as in 52 above.

80. In *stabb'd with laughter* some see an allusion to the " stitch
in the side " often caused by laughter.

82. *Encounters.* The abstract for the concrete. *Encounterers*
occurs in *T. and C.* iv. 5. 58.

87. *Saint Denis.* The patron saint of France. Cf. *Hen. V.* v.
2. 193, 220, etc. For *Saint Cupid,* cf. iv. 3. 364 above.

88. *Charge their breath against us.* Make this wordy attack
upon us.

92. *Addrest.* Directed; as in *T. N.* i. 4. 15: "address thy gait
unto her," etc.

101. *Made a doubt.* Expressed the fear.

104. *Audaciously.* Boldly, with confidence.

109. *Rubb'd his elbow.* A sign of satisfaction. Herford quotes
Jonson, *Bartholomew Fair,* iii. 1: "Oh rare! I would fain rub
my elbow now, but I dare not pull my hand." *Fleer'd* =
grinned.

117. *Spleen ridiculous.* "Ridiculous fit of laughter" (Johnson). Cf. *M. for M.* ii. 2. 122. See also iii. 1. 77 above.

118. *Passion's solemn tears.* That is, tears which are usually the expression of deep sorrow. *Passion* is often = violent sorrow; as in *Temp.* i. 2. 392, etc. See also the verb in i. 1. 260 above.

121. *Like Muscovites or Russians.* Knight remarks: "For the Russian or Muscovite habits assumed by the king and nobles of Navarre, we are indebted to Vecellio. At page 303 of the edition of 1598, we find a noble Muscovite whose attire sufficiently corresponds with that described by Hall in his account of a Russian masque at Westminster, in the reign of Henry VIII., quoted by Ritson in illustration of this play. 'In the first year of King Henry VIII.,' says the chronicler, 'at a banquet made for the foreign ambassadors in the Parliament-chamber at Westminster, came the Lord Henry Earl of Wiltshire, and the Lord Fitzwalter, in two long gowns of yellow satin traversed with white satin, and in every bend of white was a bend of crimson satin, after the fashion of Russia or Russland, with furred hats of grey on their heads, either of them having an hatchet in their hands, and boots with pikes turned up.' The boots in Vecellio's print have no 'pikes turned up,' but we perceive the 'long gown' of figured satin or damask, and the 'furred hat.' At page 283 of the same work we are presented also with the habit of the Grand Duke of Muscovy, a rich and imposing costume which might be worn by his majesty of Navarre himself." See the cut (copied from Knight) on p. 147 above.

122. *Parle.* Parley. Cf. *R. of L.* 100: "parling looks." For the noun, see *Hen. V.* iii. 3. 2, etc.

123. *Love-feat.* Plausibly altered by Dyce and others to "love-suit;" but *love-feat* may include "the various feats of parleying, courting, and dancing" (Clarke).

125. *Several.* Separate; as often. Cf. the quibble in ii. 1. 223 above.

146. *To the death.* Though death were the consequence of

refusal. Cf. *Rich. III.* iii. 2. 55 : " I will not do it, to the death."

159. *Taffeta.* The taffeta masks they wore to conceal themselves. The early eds. give this line to Biron ; corrected by Theobald.

160. *Parcel.* For the personal use, cf. *M. of V.* i. 2. 119 : "this parcel of wooers ; " and *A. W.* ii. 3. 58 : "this youthful parcel Of noble bachelors."

166. *Spirits.* Monosyllabic ; as often.

173. *Brings me out.* Puts me out. Cf. *A. Y. L.* iii. 2. 262, 265.

186. *Measure.* A grave and stately dance. Cf. *Much Ado,* ii. I. 80 : "a measure, full of state and ancientry," etc.

201. *Accompt.* For the noun, the folio has *accompt* 13 times and *account* 17 times ; the verb is always *account* (Schmidt). Cf. *compt* (= account) in *A. W.* v. 3. 57, *Macb.* i. 6. 26, etc.

207. *Eyne.* An old plural of *eye ;* found without the rhyme in *R. of L.* 1229.

209. *Request'st.* The early eds. have "requests." Second persons of verbs ending with *t* are often thus contracted.

216. *The man.* That is, the man in the moon.

220. *Nice.* Coy, prudish. Cf. iii. 1. 22 above.

222. *Curtsy.* See on i. 2. 63 above.

233. *Treys.* Threes ; as in dice and card playing.

234. *Metheglin.* A sweet beverage. Cf. *M. W.* v. 5. 167 (Evans's speech) : "Sack and wine and metheglins." *Wort* is unfermented beer.

236. *Cog.* Deceive ; specifically used of falsifying dice.

239. *Change.* Often = exchange, on which sense Maria plays just below.

248. *Veal.* Perhaps punning on the foreign pronunciation of *well* (Malone). Boswell quotes *The Wisdome of Dr. Dodypoll :* —

" *Doctor.* Hans, my very speciall friend ; fait and trot me be right glad for see you veale.

Hans. What, do you make a calfe of me, M. Doctor? "

The Cambridge editors say: "The word alluded to is *Viel*, a word which would be likely to be known from the frequent use which the sailors from Hamburg or Bremen would have cause to make of the phrase *zu viel* [too much] in their bargains with the London shopkeepers."

260. *The sense of sense.* See on i. 1. 64 above.

264. *Dry-beaten.* Cudgelled, thrashed. Cf. *R. and J.* iii. 1. 82 and iv. 5. 126. We find "dry basting" in *C. of E.* ii. 2. 64.

269. *Well-liking.* Well-conditioned. Cf. what Falstaff says in 1 *Hen. IV.* iii. 3. 6: "I'll repent, while I am in some liking" (while I have some flesh). See also *M. W.* ii. 1. 57. Steevens quotes *Job*, xxix. 4.

270. *Kingly-poor.* Poor for a king; not hyphened in the early eds. and perhaps corrupt. Perhaps Herford's explanation may be accepted: "A royal jest; one that has only its royal origin to commend it."

275. *Weeping-ripe.* Ripe for weeping, ready to weep; used again in 3 *Hen. VI.* i. 4. 172: "What, weeping-ripe, my lord Northumberland?" Cf. *reeling-ripe* in *Temp.* v. 1. 279 and *sinking-ripe* in *C. of E.* i. 1. 78.

278. *No point.* See on ii. 1. 190 above.

280. *Qualm.* Probably a play on *calm*, which seems to have been pronounced like it. Cf. 2 *Hen. IV.* ii. 4. 40: "sick of a calm."

282. *Statute-caps.* Woollen caps, which, by act of Parliament in 1571, the citizens were required to wear on Sundays and holidays. The nobility were exempt from the requirement, which, as Strype informs us, was "in behalf of the trade of cappers" — one of sundry such "protection" measures in the time of Elizabeth. The meaning evidently is, that "better wits may be found among citizens" (Steevens), or common folk.

284. *Quick.* Sprightly. See on i. 1. 161 above.

298. *Damask.* Cf. the reference to cheeks in *A. Y. L.* iii. 5. 123: "Betwixt the constant red and mingled damask."

299. *Angels vailing clouds.* That is, letting fall the clouds that have masked or hidden them. For *vail* = lower, let fall, cf. *M. of V.* i. 1. 28, *Ham.* i. 2. 70, etc. It has been often confounded with *veil* by editors and printers.

305. *Shapeless.* Unshapely, ugly; as in *R. of L.* 973 and *C. of E.* iv. 2. 20.

317. *As pigeons pease.* Steevens quotes from Ray's *Proverbs :* —

> "Children pick up words as pigeons peas,
>   And utter them again as God shall please."

318. *God.* The reading of 1st quarto, changed in the folio to "Jove;" doubtless on account of the statute against the use of the name of God on the stage.

320. *Wassails.* Drinking-bouts, carousals. Cf. *Macb.* i. 7. 64: "wine and wassail," etc.

325. *Carve.* Carving was considered a courtly accomplishment; but the word here probably has the same sense as in *M. W.* i. 3. 49: "She discourses, she carves, she gives the leer of invitation," where it refers to making certain signs with the fingers, or a kind of amorous telegraphy. On *lisp*, cf. *M. W.* iii. 3. 77: "these lisping hawthorn buds, that come like women in men's apparel," etc.

328. *Tables.* The old name for backgammon.

330. *A mean.* A tenor. Cf. *T. G. of V.* i. 2. 95: "The mean is drown'd by your unruly base;" and *W. T.* iv. 3. 46: "means and bases." Steevens quotes Bacon: "The treble cutteth the air so sharp, as it returneth too swift to make the sound equal; and therefore a mean or tenor is the sweetest."

334. *Whale's.* A dissyllable. Cf. Spenser, *F. Q.* iii. 1. 15: "And eke, through feare, as white as whales bone." The simile was a common one in the old poets, as Steevens shows by many quotations. The reference is to the tooth of the walrus, or "horse-whale," then much used as a substitute for ivory.

336. *Boyet.* The rhyme with *debt* is to be noted. Cf. p. 154 above.

342. *In all hail.* With a play on *hail* = hail-stones (Clarke).

363. *Mess.* See on iv. 3. 206, and cf. 369 below.

367. *To the manner.* According to the manner, or fashion.

368. *Undeserving praise.* Undeserved praise, or praise to the undeserving. Cf. *beholding* = beholden (regularly in S.), *all-obeying* (= obeyed by all) in *A. and C.* iii. 13. 77, etc.

376. *When we greet,* etc. That is, when we look upon the sun it dazzles or blinds our eyes.

391. *We are descried,* etc. This speech and the next are spoken aside, as is evident from what the princess says immediately after; but no former editor, so far as I am aware, has marked them so.

394. *Swoon!* The quartos and 1st folio have "sound," which was one of the ways of spelling the word. It is found in the folio in *M. N. D.* ii. 2. 154, *A. Y. L.* v. 2. 29, *Rich. III.* iv. 1. 35, *R. and J.* iii. 2. 56, etc. The later folios have "swound," which often occurs in the early eds. In *R. of L.* 1486, we find *swounds* rhyming with *wounds*. *Swown* and *swoond* (present) are other old forms.

406. *Friend.* Sometimes = mistress; as in *M. for M.* i. 4. 29: "He hath got his friend with child." For the corresponding masculine use (= paramour), see *Oth.* iv. 1. 3: "naked with her friend in bed," etc.

409. *Three pil'd.* Superfine; or like three-piled velvet, the richest kind. Cf. *M. for M.* i. 2. 33: "thou art good velvet; thou 'rt a three-piled piece;" and *W. T.* iv. 3. 14: "and in my time wore three-pile."

For *affectation* (Rowe's reading) the early eds. have "affection." See on v. 1. 4 above. White retains "affection," which he would make a quadrisyllable, rhyming with *ostentati-on*. *Hyperboles*, he says, is a trisyllable, *hy-pér-boles*, as in *T. and C.* i. 3. 161: "Would seem hyperboles. At this fusty stuff." But *ostentati-on* would make the line an alexandrine, which (see on i. 1. 108 above) S. rarely used in his early plays; and it does not seem at all necessary to make *hyperbole* a trisyllable in *T. and C. Affectation* is found in the folio in *M. W.* i. 1. 152 and *Ham.* ii. 2. 464; *affection* (in the same sense) only here and in v. 1. 4 above.

415. *Russet.* Homespun; *russet* being a common colour for such fabrics. *Kersey* was a coarse woollen stuff.

417. *Sans.* Without; a French word that had become quite Anglicized in the time of S., being used (spelt "sance" or "sanse") in French and Italian dictionaries to define *sans* and *senza*. In her reply Rosaline bids him speak without *sans*, that is, without French words.

421. '*Lord have mercy on us.*' "The inscription put upon the doors of the houses infected with the plague. The *tokens* of the plague are the first spots or discolorations by which the infection is known to be received" (Johnson). Cf. *A. and C.* iii. 10. 9: "like the token'd pestilence."

427. *States.* Estates; as not unfrequently.

429. *Being those that sue?* A play upon *sue* = prosecute by law (Johnson).

436. *Well advis'd?* Probably = in your right mind. Cf. *C. of E.* ii. 2. 215: "mad or well advis'd?" The ordinary sense of "acting with due deliberation," which most editors give here, seems rather tame.

442. *Force not.* "Make no difficulty" (Johnson), or "care not for" (Schmidt). Cf. *R. of L.* 1021: "I force not argument a straw." Collier quotes the interlude of *Jacob and Esau*, 1568: —

> "O Lorde! some good body, for Gods sake, gyve me meate,
> I force not what it were, so that I had to eate."

461. *Neither of either.* A common expression of the time, found in *The London Prodigal* and other comedies (Malone).

462. *Consent.* Compact, conspiracy.

465. *Please-man.* Pickthank, parasite; used by S. only here. A *zany* was a subordinate buffoon. Cf. *T. N.* i. 5. 96: "the fools' zanies."

466. *Trencher-knight.* Servingman. Cf. 479 below.

467. *In years.* Probably = into wrinkles, like those of age. Cf. *M. of V.* i. 1. 80: "With mirth and laughter let old wrinkles come."

473. *In will, and error.* "First wilfully, afterwards by mistake" (Clarke).

476. *Squire.* Square, or foot-rule. Cf. *W. T.* iv. 4. 348 or 1 *Hen. IV.* ii. 2. 13. There is a vulgar proverb, "He has the length of her foot" = he knows her humour exactly (Heath).

477. *Upon the apple of her eye ?* In obedience to her glance.

480. *You are allow'd.* "An allowed fool" (*T. N.* i. 5. 101), a privileged jester.

483. *Wounds like a leaden sword.* Cf. *J. C.* iii. 1. 173: "To you our swords have leaden points."

484. *Manage . . . career.* Terms of the stable and the tiltyard. On *manage*, cf. *A. Y. L.* i. 1. 13, *Hen. VIII.* v. 3. 24, etc. A *career* was an encounter of knights at full gallop. Cf. *Rich. II.* i. 2. 49, etc.

492. *You cannot beg us.* "That is, we are not fools ; our next relations cannot *beg* the wardship of our persons and fortunes. One of the legal tests of a *natural* is to try whether he can number" (Johnson). Knight remarks : "One of the most abominable corruptions of the feudal system of government was for the sovereign, who was the legal guardian of idiots, to grant the wardship of such an unhappy person to some favourite, granting with the idiot the right of using his property. Ritson, and Douce more correctly, give a curious anecdote illustrative of this custom, and of its abuse : 'The Lord North begg'd old Bladwell for a foole (though he could never prove him so), and having him in his custodie as a lunaticke, he carried him to a gentleman's house, one day, that was his neighbour. The L. North and the gentleman retir'd awhile to private discourse, and left Bladwell in the dining-roome, which was hung with a faire hanging ; Bladwell walking up and downe, and viewing the imagerie, spyed a foole at last in the hanging, and without delay drawes his knife, flyes at the foole, cutts him cleane out, and

layes him on the floore ; my Lord and the gentleman coming in
againe, and finding the tapestrie thus defac'd, he ask'd Bladwell
what he meant by such a rude uncivill act ; he answered, Sir, be
content, I have rather done you a courtesie than a wrong, for, if
ever my L. N. had seene the foole there he would have begg'd him,
and so you might have lost your whole suite ' (*Harl. MS.* 6395)."

502. *Whereuntil.* Whereunto, to what.

503. *Pursent.* For *present.* See on v. 1. 122 above.

518, 519. *Where zeal*, etc. I leave this passage as in the folio
(with the Cambridge editors), in preference to adopting any one
of the many emendations that have been proposed. The plural
contents is used for the sake of the rhyme ; and the meaning seems
to be : where zeal strives to please, but the very effort is fatal to the
pleasure. The context is the best commentary upon it.

529. *Honey.* For the personal use, cf. 1 *Hen. IV.* i. 2. 179,
T. and C. v. 2. 18, *R. and J.* ii. 5. 18, etc.

532. *Fortuna de la guerra.* Fortune of war (Spanish). Hanmer has " della guerra," forgetting that Armado is a Spaniard and
not an Italian. The early eds. have " delaguar; " and Schmidt
conjectures " del agua " (of the water, alluding to the old saying
that swimming must be tried in the water) or " de la guarda " (of
guard, " that is, guarding Fortune ").

533. *Couplement.* Used here for *couple.* In *Sonn.* 21. 5 it is =
combination.

543. *Hedge-priest.* A term of contempt for priests of the lowest
type ; like Sir Oliver Martext in *A. Y. L.* S. uses the word only
here.

545. *Novum.* Hanmer reads " novem." *Novum* (or *novem*)
was a game at dice. Steevens quotes Greene, *Art of Legerdemain*, 1612: "The principal use of them [dice] is at novum,"
etc. *Abate* = leave out, except ; and the meaning is : " except in
a throw at novum, the whole world could not furnish five such."

546. *Prick out.* Mark out. Cf. *Sonn.* 20. 13: "prick'd thee
out for women's pleasure." See also 2 *Hen. IV.* iii. 2. 121 fol.

and *J. C.* iii. 1. 216, iv. 1. 1, 16. Some eds. adopt the quarto "pick."

549. *Libbard's.* Leopard's; the knee-caps in old dresses and plate-armour often being in the form of a leopard's head (Dyce).

566. *Stand's too right.* According to Plutarch, Alexander's head had a twist towards the left. The next line alludes to the statement of the same author that Alexander's skin had "a marvellous good savour."

577. *The painted cloth.* For the historical and other paintings on the cloth hangings of rooms, cf. *A. Y. L.* iii. 2. 291, 1 *Hen. IV.* iv. 2. 28, *R. of L.* 245, etc.

578. *That holds his poll-axe*, etc. The arms of Alexander, as given in the old history of the Nine Worthies, were a lion sitting in a chair holding a battle-axe (Tollet).

579. *Ajax.* There is a play on *a jakes* (privy); a coarse joke that occurs in Jonson, Camden, Sir John Harington, and other writers of the time.

580. *Afeard.* The quarto has *afeard*, and the folios *afraid*. The forms are used interchangeably in the early eds.

585. *A little o'erparted.* With a *part*, or *rôle*, a little too much for him.

589. *Imp.* Youngster. See on i. 2. 5 above.

590. *Canus.* Dog (Latin *canis*); the reading in the early eds., which may be retained for the sake of the rhyme.

599. *Ycliped.* Yclept; mispronounced for the sake of the joke that follows.

611. *A cittern-head.* A *cittern* (cithern, gittern, or guitar) often had a grotesque face carved upon its *head*.

616. *Flask.* That is, a powder-flask; as in *R. and J.* iii. 3. 132.

617. *Half-cheek in a brooch.* Profile on a clasp, or buckle. Cf. *half-face* in *K. John*, i. 1. 92.

631. *Baited!* Worried; like a *baited* bear or bull.

634. *Come home by me.* That is, come home to me.

636. *Trojan.* The early eds. have "Troyan," as often else-where. The word was much used as a term of contempt. See 1 *Hen. IV.* ii. 1. 77, *Hen. V.* v. 1. 20, 23, etc.

638. *Clean-timbered.* Well-built; used by S. nowhere else.

641. *The small.* That is, of the leg.

645. *Lances.* Lancers; as in *Lear*, v. 3. 50: "our impress'd lances," etc.

647. *A gilt nutmeg.* Mentioned by Jonson in his *Christmas Masque* as a present (Steevens). An orange or lemon, *stuck with cloves*, was a common new-year's gift.

654. *Breath'd.* Endowed with breath, or "wind;" in full vigour. Cf. *A. and C.* iii. 13. 178: "treble-sinew'd, hearted, breath'd."

665. After this line Capell gives the stage-direction, "*Biron steps to Costard and whispers him;*" that is, putting him up to the trick on Armado.

671. *This Hector*, etc. Dyce, who adopts Capell's stage-direction at 665 just above, has here "*Costard [suddenly coming from behind]*. The party is gone," etc. White, who makes Costard leave at 589 above, has at 665 "*Birone goes out*," and here "*Enter* COSTARD *hastily and unarmed, and* BIRONE *after him.*" It is doubtful just how the trick was meant to be managed, and any one of the ways suggested by the editors would do well enough on the stage. It could safely be left to the actors without any stage-direction, as in the Cambridge ed.

680. *Quick by him.* There is a play on *quick* = alive. Cf. *Ham.* v. 1. 137: "'T is for the dead, not for the quick," etc. See also *Acts*, x. 42, etc.

687. *More Ates!* "That is, more instigation. *Ate* was the mis-chievous goddess that incited bloodshed" (Johnson). Cf. *Much Ado*, ii. 1. 263, *K. John*, ii. 1. 63, and *J. C.* iii. 1. 271.

693. *Fight with a pole*, etc. That is, with the quarter-staff, a long pole in the use of which the men of the North of England were skilful. It was used chiefly by the peasantry.

695. *My arms.* "The weapons and armour which he wore in his character of Pompey" (Johnson).

699. *Let me take you*, etc. "Perhaps = let me speak without ceremony" (Schmidt).

709. *Woolward.* That is, with woollen next to the skin, or without linen. Grey quotes Stowe's *Annals:* "he went woolward and barefooted to many churches, in every of them to pray to God for help in his blindness." Farmer adds from Lodge's *Incarnate Devils,* 1596: "His common course is to go always untrust [untrussed]; except when his shirt is a washing, and then he goes woolward."

721. *I have seen*, etc. "Armado means to say in his affected style, that he had discovered that he was wronged, and was determined to right himself as a soldier" (Mason). "One may see day at a little hole" is found in Ray's *Proverbs. Through the little hole of discretion* may be = "though discreetly forbearing from righting myself until I can do it with dignity," as Steevens and Clarke explain it.

731. *Liberal.* Too free, over-bold. It is used in a yet stronger sense in *Much Ado,* iv. 1. 93: "a liberal villain," etc.

733. *Converse of breath.* That is, in conversation. For the accent of *converse,* cf. *Oth.* iii. 1. 40. Steevens compares *M. of V.* v. 1. 141: "this breathing courtesy" (these courteous words).

735. *Humble.* Apparently = obsequious, formal, polite. Many eds. follow Theobald in reading "nimble." Cf. *humble* in 629 above. "The princess means to say that when the heart is heavy the tongue is not apt to find polite words in which to acknowledge a great benefit" — referring to the granting of her suit about Aquitaine and the ransom.

738. *The extreme parts of time*, etc. I retain the folio reading, which Dr. B. Nicholson (*Trans. of New. Shaks. Soc.* for 1874, p. 513) explains thus: "The *extreme parts* are the end parts, *extremities* — as, of our body, the fingers; of chains, the final links; of given portions of time, the last of those units into which we choose

to divide them. Afterwards (in 85) the King, representing the stay of the Princess as for an hour, calls *the extreme part* 'the latest minute,' and the thought in both passages is so far the same. It is not however said that our decision is necessitated by the extremity of the moment, though this is perhaps suggested to us by the sound of the words used; but that concurring circumstances, and therefore *Time*, as the producer of those circumstances, so influence our decision that he, and not we, may be called the decider. Hence Time, as personified, and as the intelligential agent of whom the extreme parts are but the instrumental members, is considered as the true nominative to the verb *forms*, and is represented as fashioning or moulding all causes or questions to the purposes of his speed, that is, to his own intents, or to those of the fate or Providence of which he is the sub-agent. This thought has been forced upon the King by finding that his high resolves of study were at once broken by the coming of the Princess, while her sudden departure shows him that he cannot do without her love; and he urges it as an excuse for the intrusion of his love on her time of grief, and as an excuse for her favourable reply.

"In the next lines, though still personifying Time, the King changes his illustration. Often the archer may weigh variously all the circumstances — the bow, the arrow, the intended strength of shot and elevation, the wind and the like — and so vary from moment to moment; but *at the very loose*, or loosing of the shaft (an act the proper doing of which was much dwelt on by archers) he comes to a quick and determined decision. 'So during your stay, princess,' says the King, 'I and my lords acted doubtfully between our former resolves and our new loves, and you have dallied with us: now at your departure, at the last moment, I decide and ask your love; do you answer with the same determinateness.' In retort, the Princess most consistently decides in accord with the events which Time has purposed in her regard, for the declaration of the King is only one of these, another and the first being the news of her father's death.

"The thought of the first two lines is allied and similar to Hamlet's

> ' There 's a divinity that shapes our ends,
> Rough-hew them as we will; '

just as the rest expresses the similar idea specially illustrated in the catastrophe of that play.   But here the subject being of a gentler nature, the King speaks more conversationally and less reflectively than Hamlet does, and of *Time* and not of a Providence or *divinity*."

Forms has been changed to "form," but quite unnecessarily. Cf. iv. 3. 342 above.

Extreme is accented on the first syllable because preceding the noun.   See on *profound*, in iv. 3. 166 above.

744. *Convince.* Overcome, conquer.   Cf. *Macb.* i. 7. 64, iv. 3. 142, *Oth.* iv. 1. 28, etc.

750. *Dull.* The early eds. have "double," which is clearly corrupt.   Some read "hear dully."

758. *Strains.* Impulses, vagaries.   Cf. *M. W.* ii. 1. 91, *T. of A.* iv. 3. 213, etc.

759. *Skipping.* Flighty, frivolous.   Cf. *M. of V.* ii. 2. 196: —

> " Pray thee, take pain
> To allay with some cold drops of modesty
> Thy skipping spirit, lest through thy wild behaviour
> I be misconstrued," etc.

766. *Have misbecom'd.* The "confusion of construction" is like many other instances in S.   For the form *misbecom'd*, cf. *becomed* in *R. and J.* iv. 2. 26, *A. and C.* iii. 7. 26, and *Cymb.* v. 5. 406.

768. *Suggested.* Tempted ; as in *Oth.* ii. 3. 358: —

> " When devils will the blackest sins put on,
> They do suggest at first with heavenly shows."

Cf. *suggestions* in i. 1. 158 above.

779. *Bombast.* Originally, *cotton* used to stuff out garments. Cf. the quotation from Stubbes in note on iii. 1. 17 above.   Gerarde, in his *Herbal*, calls the cotton plant "the bombast tree ; "

and Lupton, in *A Thousand Notable Things*, speaks of a candle
" with a wick of bumbast."

780. *Respects* = considerations, thoughts.

784. *Quote.* Construe, interpret. Cf. *misquote* = misconstrue,
in 1 *Hen. IV.* v. 2. 13, the only instance of the word in S. See
also ii. 1. 245 above.

787. *World-without-end.* Cf. *Sonn.* 57. 5 : —

> " Nor dare I chide the world-without-end hour
> Whilst I, my sovereign, watch the clock for you."

789. *Dear.* Used in an intensive sense ; as in 862 below. See
also on ii. 1. 1 above.

799. *Weeds.* Garments ; as often.

801. *Last love.* " Continue to be love " (Steevens).

812. *Flatter up.* For the *up*, see on iv. 3. 303 above. The
meaning is : " in order that I might soothe or pamper these facul-
ties of mine by leading a life of repose " (Clarke).

815–820. *And what . . . sick.* Evidently a part of the first
sketch which was rewritten in revising the play. See on iv. 3.
297 above.

816. *Rank.* Cf. *Ham.* iii. 3. 36 : " O, my offence is rank," etc.

817. *Attaint.* Attainted. Such contractions of participles ending in *t* (*acquit, addict, quit,* etc.) are common. We find *taint* in
1 *Hen. VI.* v. 3. 183 : " heart never yet taint with love."

822. *A wife ?* The early eds. give this to Katherine, reading :
" A wife? a beard, faire health," etc. Dyce was the first to trans-
fer *A wife ?* to Dumain, in whose mouth it seems more natural.

843. *All estates.* All kinds or conditions of people ; as in
Rich. III. iii. 7. 213 : " And equally, indeed, to all estates." Latimer, in his *Sermons*, says it is the duty of a king " to see to all
estates, to provide for the poor," etc.

851. *Fierce.* Ardent, strenuous ; as in *Lear*, ii. 1. 36, etc.

855. *Agony.* " Used specifically ; the death-throes " (Herford).

862. *Dear.* See on 789 above.

867. *Reformation.* Metrically five syllables.

871. *Bring you.* Accompany you. Cf. *W. T.* iv. 3. 122: "Shall I bring thee on the way?" See also *Genesis*, xviii. 16, *Acts*, xxi. 5, 2 *Corinthians*, i. 16, etc.

873. *Jack hath not Jill.* Cf. *M. N. D.* iii. 2. 461: "Jack shall have Jill," etc.

892. *Pied.* Variegated. Cf. *M. of V.* i. 3. 80: "streak'd and pied," etc.

893. *Lady-smocks.* Ellacombe (*Plant-Lore of S.*) says: "*Lady-smocks* are the flowers of *Cardamine pratensis*, the pretty early meadow flower of which children are so fond, and of which the popularity is shown by its many names, Lady-smocks, Cuckoo-flower, Meadow Cress, Pinks, Spinks, Bog-spinks, and May-flower, and 'in Northfolke, Canterbury Bells.' The origin of the name is not very clear. It is generally explained from the resemblance of the flowers to smocks hung out to dry, but the resemblance seems to me rather far-fetched. According to another explanation, 'the Lady-smock, a corruption of Our Lady's-smock, is so called from its first flowering about Lady-tide. It is a pretty purplish-white, tetradynamous plant, which blows from Lady-tide till the end of May, and which during the latter end of April covers the moist meadows with its silvery-white, which looks at a distance like a white sheet spread over the fields' (*Circle of the Seasons*). Those who adopt this view called the plant Our Lady's-smock, but I cannot find that name in any old writers. Drayton, coeval with Shakespeare, says: —

'Some to grace the show,
Of Lady-smocks most white do rob each neighbouring meed,
Wherewith their loose locks most curiously they braid.'

And Isaac Walton, in the next century, drew that pleasant picture of himself sitting quietly by the waterside — 'looking down the meadows I could see here a boy gathering Lilies and Lady-smocks, and there a girl cropping Culverkeys and Cowslips.'"

894. *Cuckoo-buds.* "There is a difficulty in deciding what flower Shakespeare meant by Cuckoo-buds. We now always give the name to the Meadow Cress (*Cardamine pratensis*), but it cannot be that in either of these passages, because that flower is mentioned under its other name of Lady-smocks in the previous line, nor is it 'of yellow hue;' nor does it grow among Corn, as described in *Lear*, iv. 4. 4. Many plants have been suggested, but I think the Buttercup, as suggested by Dr. Prior, will best meet the requirements" (Ellacombe).

897. *Mocks married men.* The note of the *cuckoo* was thought to prognosticate cuckoldom. Cf. *M. N. D.* iii. 1. 134 and *A. W.* i. 3. 67.

903. *Turtles.* Turtle-doves. See on iv. 3. 210 above.

910. *Hang by the wall.* That is, from the eaves. Malone compares *Hen. V.* iii. 5. 23 and *Temp.* v. 1. 17.

911. *Blows his nail.* To warm his fingers. Cf. 3 *Hen. VI.* ii. 5. 3: "the shepherd, blowing of his nails." See also *T. of S.* i. 1. 109.

918. *Keel.* Cool; that is, by stirring it. Clarke says the word came also to mean skimming off the scum that rose to the top, which may be the sense here. Collier quotes *Piers Plowman:* —

> "And lerede men a ladel bygge, with a long stele
> That caste for to kele a crockke, and save the fatte above;"

that is, they skimmed the crock, or pot, with a ladle, in order to save the fat. Schmidt also defines *keel* as "to scum (German *kielen*)."

920. *Saw.* Moral saying, maxim. Cf. *A. Y. L.* ii. 7. 156: "Full of wise saws;" 2 *Hen. VI.* i. 3. 61: "holy saws of sacred writ," etc.

923. *Crabs.* Crab-apples; often roasted and put into the wassail-bowl. Cf. *M. N. D.* ii. 1. 48 (Puck's speech): —

> "And sometime lurk I in a gossip's bowl,
> In very likeness of a roasted crab."

APPENDIX

SHAKESPEARE AND FLORIO

JOHN FLORIO was born in London about 1553, and died full of years and honours in 1625, having survived Shakespeare nine years. He had married the sister of Daniel the poet, and Ben Jonson presented a copy of *The Fox* to him, with the inscription, "To his loving father and worthy friend Master John Florio, Ben Jonson seals this testimony of his friendship and love." Daniel writes a poem of some length in praise of Florio's translation of Montaigne, while other contemporary poets contribute commendatory verses which are prefixed to his other publications. A sonnet prefixed to his *Second Frutes* (a book of Italian-English dialogues for students) has been ascribed by Professor Minto and others to Shakespeare. In a subsequent work Florio refers to this sonnet as the production of a friend "who loved better to be a poet than to be called one," and vindicates it from the indirect attack of a hostile critic, H. S., who had also disparaged the work in which it appeared ; but I am inclined to agree with H. S. rather than with Florio or Minto, and cannot believe that Shakespeare wrote it.

In the British Museum there is a copy of Florio's *Montaigne* (1603) with Shakespeare's name on the fly-leaf, but experts are not agreed that it is his autograph. We know, however, that the dramatist had read Florio's book, for Gonzalo's description of his ideal republic in *The Tempest* (ii. 1. 144 fol.) is little else than a paraphrase of this passage in it: "It is a nation, would I answere Plato, that hath no kindle of traffike, no knowledge of Letters, no intelligence of numbers, no name of magistrate, nor of politike superioritie ; no use of service, of riches, or of povertie ; no contracts, no

219

successions, no partitions, no occupation, but idle; no respect of
kindred but common; no apparell but naturall; no manuring of
lands; no use of wine, corn, or mettle. The very words that import lying, falsehood, treason, dissimulation, covetousness, envie,
detraction, and pardon were never heard of amongst them."

Shakespeare's rendering of it may be added, to save the reader
the trouble of referring to the play: —

> "*Gonzalo.* I' the commonwealth I would by contraries
> Execute all things; for no kind of traffic
> Would I admit; no name of magistrate;
> Letters should not be known; riches, poverty,
> And use of service, none; contract, succession,
> Bourn, bound of land, tilth, vineyard, none;
> No use of metal, corn, or wine, or oil;
> No occupation; all men idle, all;
> And women too, but innocent and pure;
> No sovereignty; —
>> *Sebastian.*   Yet he would be king on 't.
>> *Antonio.* The latter end of his commonwealth forgets the
>>   beginning.
>> *Gonzalo.* All things in common nature should produce
> Without sweat or endeavour; treason, felony,
> Sword, pike, knife, gun, or need of any engine,
> Would I not have; but nature should bring forth,
> Of it own kind, all foison, all abundance,
> To feed my innocent people."

Baynes remarks: "The *First Fruits* was published in 1578, and
was for some years the most popular manual for the study of Italian. It is the book that Shakespeare would naturally have used
in attempting to acquire a knowledge of the language after his
arrival in London; and on finding that the author was the friend
of some of his literary associates he would probably have sought
his acquaintance and secured his personal help. As Florio was
also a French scholar and habitually taught both languages, Shakespeare probably owed to him his knowledge of French as well as

of Italian. . . . In any case Shakespeare would almost certainly have met Florio a few years later at the house of Lord Southampton, with whom the Italian scholar seems to have occasionally resided. It also appears that he was in the habit of visiting at several titled houses, among others those of the Earl of Bedford and Sir John Harrington. It seems also probable that he may have assisted Harrington in his translation of Ariosto. Another and perhaps even more direct link connecting Shakespeare with Florio during his early years in London is found in their common relation to the family of Lord Derby. In the year 1585 Florio translated a letter of news from Rome, giving an account of the sudden death of Pope Gregory XIII. and the election of his successor. This translation, published in July, 1585, was dedicated 'To the Right Excellent and Honourable Lord, Henry, Earl of Derby,' in terms expressive of Florio's strong personal obligations to the earl and devotion to his service. Three years later, on the death of Leicester in 1588, Lord Derby's eldest son, Ferdinando, Lord Strange, became the patron of Leicester's company of players, which Shakespeare had recently joined. The new patron must have taken special interest in the company, as they soon became (chiefly through his influence) great favourites at Court, superseding the Queen's players, and enjoying something like a practical monopoly of royal representations. Shakespeare would thus have the opportunity of making Florio's acquaintance at the outset of his London career, and everything tends to show that he did not miss the chance of numbering amongst his personal friends so accomplished a scholar, so alert, energetic, and original a man of letters, as the 'resolute John Florio.' Warburton, it is well known, suggested, or rather asserted, that Florio was the original of Holofernes in *Love's Labour's Lost*. Of all Warburton's arbitrary conjectures and dogmatic assumptions this is perhaps the most infelicitous. That a scholar and man of the world like Florio, with marked literary powers of his own, the intimate friend and associate of some of the most eminent poets of the day, living in

princely and noble circles, honoured by royal personages and wel-
comed at noble houses, — that such a man should be selected as
the original of a rustic pedant and dominie like Holofernes is surely
the climax of reckless guesswork and absurd suggestion."

As I have said elsewhere, there is no good reason to suppose
that Shakespeare ever caricatured any particular person anywhere
in his works. Allibone, following Drake and certain other commentators, says that Florio offended the dramatists of his day by
declaring that "the plaies that they do plaie in England are
neither *right comedies* nor *right tragedies*, but representations of
histories without any decorum," and that Shakespeare "retaliated
this assault by ridiculing Florio in the character of Holofernes."
Brewer, in his *Dictionary of Phrase and Fable*, says, in addition to
this, that the name Holofernes is an imperfect anagram for " Joh'nes
Floreo ; " and Wheeler, in his *Dictionary of Noted Names of Fic-
tion*, echoes this absurd statement. It is proved to be absurd by
the fact, also given by Wheeler, that Holofernes is the name of
the pedant who is the teacher of Gargantua in the well-known
romance by Rabelais, who died before Shakespeare was born.
That Shakespeare had read Rabelais is evident from the allusion
in *As You Like It* (iii. 2. 238), where Celia, in reply to the " Answer me in one word," with which Rosalind winds up her string of
questions about Orlando, says, " You must borrow me Gargantua's
mouth first ; 't is a word too great for any mouth of this age's size."

" Love's Labour's Lost " and Tennyson's " Princess "

Not a few critics have suggested that Tennyson got the hint of
the plot of *The Princess* from *Love's Labour's Lost;* and this is
certainly possible, though, as Mr. Boas remarks (*Shakspere and his
Predecessors*, 1896), the theme, " in one form or other, is as old
as life itself." He adds : " In our own day it is generally women
rather than men whom the poet or the satirist depicts as rebellious

against nature's decrees, and intent upon the reversal of the primary social conditions. Foremost among such pictures is Tennyson's *Princess*, which seems to owe some of its machinery to Shakspere's play. The Princess herself, with her two chief ladies, set over against the Prince and his companions, reminds us of the grouping of characters in *Love's Labour's Lost*, the 'College' corresponds to the 'Academe,' and the oath of renunciation is in either case taken for three years. Of course, Tennyson, with 'sweet girl-graduates' as his theme, has opportunities for dainty vignettes, for piquant contrasts between the flush and glow of budding womanhood and the grey tones of academic life, which are denied to Shakspere, but the underlying ideas of both poets that love is greater than learning, and that the one sex cannot do without the other, are absolutely the same."

The Time-Analysis of the Play

This is given by Mr. P. A. Daniel, in his paper "On the Times or Durations of the Action of Shakspere's Plays" (*Trans. of New Shaks. Soc.* 1877–79, p. 145) as follows : —

"*Day* 1. — The first day of the action includes Acts I. and II. In it the Princess of France has her first interview with the King of Navarre. Toward the end of Act II. certain documents required for the establishment of the French claims are stated to have not yet come ; but, says Boyet, '*to-morrow* you shall have a sight of them,' and the King tells the Princess — '*To-morrow* shall we visit you again.'

"*Day* 2. — Act III. Armado intrusts Costard with a letter to Jaquenetta ; immediately afterwards Biron also intrusts him with a letter for Rosaline, which he is to deliver *this afternoon*.

"Act IV. sc. i. The Princess remarks that '*to-day* we shall have our dispatch.' This fixes the scene as the *morrow* referred to in the first day. Costard now enters to deliver, as he supposes, the

letter intrusted to him by Biron.   He mistakes, however, and gives
up Armado's letter to Jaquenetta.

   " Act IV. sc. ii. Costard and Jaquenetta come to Holofernes
and Nathaniel to get them to read the letter, as they suppose, of
Armado to Jaquenetta.   It turns out to be the letter of Biron to
Rosaline, and Costard and Jaquenetta are sent off to give it up at
once to the King.   It is clear that these scenes from the beginning
of Act III. are all on one day ; but at the end of this scene Holofernes invites Nathaniel and Dull to *dine* with him 'to-day at the
father's of a pupil of mine.'   This does not agree very well with
' this afternoon' mentioned in Act III., and one or the other — the
afternoon, I think — must be set down as an oversight.

   " Act IV. sc. iii. Still the same day. The King, Longaville, and
Dumain mutually detect each other of love, and Biron triumphs
over all three till his own backslidings are exposed by the entry
of Costard and Jaquenetta with his letter to Rosaline.   Finally, all
four resolve to woo their mistresses openly, and determine that —

                         ' —— in the *afternoon*
          [They] will with some strange pastime solace them.'

   " In pursuance of this idea in the next scene, Act V. sc. i., we
find Armado consulting Holofernes and Nathaniel — who have now
returned from their dinner — as to some masque with which ' it is
the King's most sweet pleasure and affection to congratulate the
Princess at her pavilion in the posteriors of this day, which the rude
multitude call the afternoon.'   A masque of the Nine Worthies is
determined on.

   " In the next scene the masque is presented accordingly, and
with this scene the Play ends.

   " The time of the action, then, is two days :

   " 1. Acts I. and II.

   " 2. Acts III. to V."

LIST OF CHARACTERS IN THE PLAY

The numbers in parenthesis indicate the lines the characters have in each scene.

King: i. 1(117); ii. 1(47); iv. 3(76); v. 2(82). Whole no. 322.

Biron: i. 1(128); ii. 1(18); iii. 1(51); iv. 3(237); v. 2(193). Whole no. 627.

Longaville: i. 1(14); ii. 1 (6); iv. 3(33); v. 2(17). Whole no. 70.

Dumain: i. 1(8); ii. 1(2); iv. 3(44); v. 2(37). Whole no. 91.

Boyet: ii. 1(67); iv. 1(64); v. 2(103). Whole no. 234.

Mercade: v. 2(4). Whole no. 4.

Armado: i. 2(96); iii. 1(58); v. 1(48), 2(53). Whole no. 255.

Nathaniel: iv. 2(45); v. 1(13), 2(22). Whole no. 80.

Holofernes: iv. 2(104); v. 1(60), 2(36). Whole no. 200.

Dull: i. 1(9), 2(7); iv. 2(13); v. 1(3). Whole no. 32.

Costard: i. 1(44), 2(13); iii. 1(40); iv. 1(26), 2(3), 3(4); v. 1(14), 2(58). Whole no. 202.

Moth: i. 2(70); iii. 1(60); v. 1(24), 2(14). Whole no. 168.

Forester: iv. 1(5). Whole no. 5.

1st Lord: ii. 1(2). Whole no. 2.

Princess: ii. 1(67); iv. 1(50); v. 2(172). Whole no. 289.

Rosaline: ii. 1(30); iv. 1(11); v. 2(137). Whole no. 178.

Maria: ii. 1(22); iv. 1(4); v. 2(16). Whole no. 42.

Katherine: ii. 1(8); v. 2(38). Whole no. 46.

Jaquenetta: i. 2(6); iv. 2(8), 3(4). Whole no. 18.

In the above enumeration parts of lines are counted as whole lines, making the total of the play greater than it is. The actual number of lines in each scene (Globe edition numbering) is as follows : i. 1(318), 2(192); ii. 1(258); iii. 1(207); iv. 1(151), 2(173), 3(386); v. 1(162), 2(942). Whole number in the play, 2789.

INDEX OF WORDS AND PHRASES EXPLAINED

INTRODUCTORY COURSE IN ARGUMENTATION

By FRANCES M. PERRY, Instructor in English in Wellesley College.

AN INTRODUCTORY COURSE IN ARGUMENTATION is intended for those who have not previously studied the subject, but while it makes a firm foundation for students who may wish to continue it, the volume is complete in itself. It is adapted for use in the first years of college or in the upper classes of secondary schools.

¶ The subject has been simplified as much as has been possible without lessening its educative value, yet no difficulties have been slighted. The beginner is set to work to exercise his reasoning power on familiar material and without the added difficulty of research. Persuasion has not been considered until conviction is fully understood. The two methods in use in teaching argumentation—the brief-drawing method and the syllogistic method—have been combined, so that the one will help the student to grasp the other.

¶ The volume is planned and proportioned with the expectation that it will be closely followed as a text-book rather than used to supplement an independent method of presentation. To that end each successive step is given explicit exposition and full illustration, and carefully graded exercises are provided to test the student's understanding of an idea, and fix it in his memory.

¶ The course is presented in three divisions; the first relating to finding and formulating the proposition for argument, the second to proving the proposition, and the last, to finding the material to prove the proposition—research.

AMERICAN BOOK COMPANY

(S. 103)

INTRODUCTORY COURSE
IN EXPOSITION

By FRANCES M. PERRY, Associate Professor of Rhetoric and Composition, Wellesley College.

EXPOSITION is generally admitted to be the most commonly used form of discourse, and its successful practice develops keen observation, deliberation, sound critical judgment, and clear and concise expression. Unfortunately, however, expository courses often fail to justify the prevailing estimate of the value of exposition, because the subject has been presented in an unsystematized manner without variety or movement.

¶ The aim of this book is to provide a systematized course in the theory and practice of expository writing. The student will acquire from its study a clear understanding of exposition — its nature ; its two processes, definition and analysis ; its three functions, impersonal presentation or transcript, interpretation, and interpretative presentation ; and the special application of exposition in literary criticism. He will also gain, through the practice required by the course, facility in writing in a clear and attractive way the various types of exposition. The volume includes an interesting section on literary criticism.

¶ The method used is direct exposition, amply reinforced by examples and exercises. The illustrative matter is taken from many and varied sources, but much of it is necessarily modern. The book meets the needs of students in the final years of secondary schools, or the first years of college.

A MERICAN BOOK COMPANY
(S.93)

NINETEENTH CENTURY ENGLISH PROSE
Critical Essays

Edited with Introductions and Notes by **THOMAS H. DICKINSON**, Ph.D., and **FREDERICK W. ROE**, **A.M.**, Assistant Professors of English, University of Wisconsin.

THIS book for college classes presents a series of ten selected essays, which are intended to trace the development of English criticism in the nineteenth century. The essays cover a definite period, and exhibit the individuality of each author's method of criticism. In each case they are those most typical of the author's critical principles, and at the same time representative of the critical tendencies of his age. The subject-matter provides interesting material for intensive study and class room discussion, and each essay is an example of excellent, though varying, style.

¶ They represent not only the authors who write, but the authors who are treated. The essays provide the best things that have been said by England's critics on Swift, on Scott, on Macaulay, and on Emerson.

¶ The introductions and notes provide the necessary biographical matter, suggestive points for the use of the teacher in stimulating discussion of the form or content of the essays, and such aids as will eliminate those matters of detail that might prove stumbling blocks to the student. Though the essays are in chronological order, they may be treated at random according to the purposes of the teacher.

AMERICAN BOOK COMPANY
(S.80)

HALLECK'S NEW ENGLISH LITERATURE

By REUBEN POST HALLECK, M. A., LL. D.
author of History of English Literature, and History of American Literature.

THIS New English Literature preserves the qualities which have caused the author's former History of English Literature to be so widely used; namely, suggestiveness, clearness, organic unity, interest, and power to awaken thought and to stimulate the student to further reading.

¶ Here are presented the new facts which have recently been brought to light, and the new points of view which have been adopted. More attention is paid to recent writers. The present critical point of view concerning authors, which has been brought about by the new social spirit, is reflected. Many new and important facts concerning the Elizabethan theater and the drama of Shakespeare's time are incorporated.

¶ Other special features are the unusually detailed Suggested Readings that follow each chapter, suggestions and references for a literary trip to England, historical introductions to the chapters, careful treatment of the modern drama, and a new and up-to-date bibliography.

¶ Over 200 pictures selected for their pedagogical value and their unusual character appear in their appropriate places in connection with the text. The frontispiece, in colors, shows the performance of an Elizabethan play in the Fortune Theater.

AMERICAN BOOK COMPANY
(S. 90)

A HISTORY OF AMERICAN LITERATURE

By REUBEN POST HALLECK, M.A.,
Principal, Male High School, Louisville, Ky.

A COMPANION volume to the author's History of English Literature. It describes the greatest achievements in American literature from colonial times to the present, placing emphasis not only upon men, but also upon literary movements, the causes of which are thoroughly investigated. Further, the relation of each period of American literature to the corresponding epoch of English literature has been carefully brought out—and each period is illuminated by a brief survey of its history. ¶ The seven chapters of the book treat in succession of Colonial Literature, The Emergence of a Nation (1754-1809), the New York Group, The New England Group, Southern Literature, Western Literature, and the Eastern Realists. To these are added a supplementary list of less important authors and their chief works, as well as A Glance Backward, which emphasizes in brief compass the most important truths taught by American literature. ¶ At the end of each chapter is a summary which helps to fix the period in mind by briefly reviewing the most significant achievements. This is followed by extensive historical and literary references for further study, by a very helpful list of suggested readings, and by questions and suggestions, designed to stimulate the student's interest and enthusiasm, and to lead him to study and investigate further for himself the remarkable literary record of American aspiration and accomplishment.

AMERICAN BOOK COMPANY

(S.318)

ROLFE'S ENGLISH CLASSICS

Edited by WILLIAM J. ROLFE, Litt. D.

BROWNING'S SELECT POEMS

Twenty poems (including "Pippa Passes"), with Introduction,
Life of Browning, Chronological Table of His Works, List of Books
useful in studying them, Critical Comments, and Notes.

BROWNING'S SELECT DRAMAS

"A Blot in the 'Scutcheon," "Colombe's Birthday," and
"A Soul's Tragedy"—with Introduction, Critical Comments,
and Notes.

GOLDSMITH'S SELECT POEMS

"The Traveller," "The Deserted Village," and "Retaliation,"
with Life of Goldsmith, Recollections and Criticisms by Thackeray,
Coleman the Younger, Campbell, Forster, and Irving, and Notes.

GRAY'S SELECT POEMS

The "Elegy," "The Bard," "The Progress of Poesy," and
other Poems, with Life of Gray, William Howitt's Description of
Stoke-Pogis, and historical, critical, and explanatory Notes.

MACAULAY'S LAYS OF ANCIENT ROME

With the Author's Preface and Introductions, Criticisms by John
Stuart Mill, Henry Morley, "Christopher North," and others,
historical and explanatory Notes, and copious Illustrations.

MILTON'S MINOR POEMS

All of Milton's Minor Poems except the Translations, with biographical and critical Introductions, and historical and explanatory Notes.

WORDSWORTH'S SELECT POEMS

Seventy-one Poems, with Life, Criticisms from Matthew Arnold,
R. H. Hutton, Principal Shairp, J. R. Lowell, and Papers of the
Wordsworth Society, and very full Notes. Illustrated by Abbey,
Parsons, and other eminent artists.

AMERICAN BOOK COMPANY

(S. 96)

NEW ROLFE SHAKESPEARE

Edited by WILLIAM J. ROLFE, Litt.D.

40 volumes, each

THE popularity of Rolfe's Shakespeare has been extraordinary. Since its first publication in 1870-83 it has been used more widely, both in schools and colleges, and by the general reading public, than any similar edition ever issued. It is to-day the standard annotated edition of Shakespeare for educational purposes.

¶ As teacher and lecturer Dr. Rolfe has been constantly in touch with the recent notable advances made in Shakespearian investigation and criticism ; and this revised edition he has carefully adjusted to present conditions.

¶ The introductions and appendices have been entirely rewritten, and now contain the history of the plays and poems; an account of the sources of the plots, with copious extracts from the chronicles and novels from which the poet drew his material ; and general comments by the editor, with selections from the best English and foreign criticism.

¶ The notes are very full, and include all the historical, critical, and illustrative material needed by the teacher, as well as by the student, and general reader. Special features in the notes are the extent to which Shakespeare is made to explain himself by parallel passages from his works; the frequent Bible illustrations; the full explanations of allusions to the manners and customs of the period; and descriptions of the localities connected with the poet's life and works.

¶ New notes have also been substituted for those referring to other volumes of the edition, so that each volume is now absolutely complete in itself. The form of the books has been modified, the page being made smaller to adjust them to pocket use.

AMERICAN BOOK COMPANY

(S. 97)

MASTERPIECES OF THE ENGLISH DRAMA

Edited under the supervision of FELIX E. SCHELLING,
Ph.D., LL.D., Professor of History and English
Literature, University of Pennsylvania.

Marlowe (Phelps)	Middleton (Sampson)
Chapman (Ellis)	Massinger (Sherman)
Beaumont and Fletcher (Schelling)	Webster and Tourneur (Thorndike)
Jonson (Rhys)	Congreve (Archer)
Goldsmith and Sheridan (Demmon)	

THIS series presents the principal dramatists, covering English dramatic history from Marlowe's Tamburlaine in 1587 to Sheridan's School for Scandal in 1777. Each volume contains four or five plays, selected with reference to their actual worth and general interest, and also because they represent the best efforts of their authors in the different varieties of dramas chosen.

¶ The texts follow the authoritative old editions, but with such occasional departures as the results of recent critical scholarship demand. Spelling and punctuation have been modernized, and obsolete and occasional words referred to the glossaries. This makes the volumes suitable for the average reader as well as for the advanced scholar.

¶ Each volume is furnished with an introduction by a British or an American scholar of rank dealing with the dramatist and his work. Each volume contains a brief biographical note, and each play is preceded by an historical note, its source, date of composition, and other kindred matters. Adequate notes are furnished at the end.

AMERICAN BOOK COMPANY

(S. 100)